The Meaning of DREAMS

The Meaning of Dreams
Calvin S. Hall
Director, Institute of Dream Research

with a new introduction by the author

McGraw-Hill Book Company
New York   Toronto   London   Sydney

For IRENE and DOVRE

Contents

The Meaning of DREAMS

INTRODUCTION for a new edition.*

THE MEANING OF DREAMS was originally published in 1953, a year that was to prove notable in the history of dreams. It was in that year that two University of Chicago scientists, Eugene Aserinsky and Nathaniel Kleitman, announced the discovery of an objective indicator of dreaming. The indicator consisted of periodic bursts of rapid, coordinated movements of the two eyes of a sleeping person. The eyes moved as if they were inspecting a visual scene, an assumption that later research was to confirm by establishing a correlation between eye movements and events in the dream. The dreamer seemed to be watching his own dream! In fact, if one watches the eyes of a sleeping person with the eyelids taped back, it appears for all the world as though he were awake and looking around in a perfectly natural way.

Within a short time, another indicator was discovered, namely, a type of brain wave characterized by low voltage and fast frequency. This type of brain wave ordinarily occurs in conjunction with rapid eye movements. Soon laboratories all over the United States, and some in other countries,

* The preparation of this introduction was supported by a USPHS research grant, MH 10207-02 from the National Institute of Mental Health, Public Health Service.

were engaged in investigating this unique stage of sleep using the electro-encephalograph (EEG) as the chief instrument for invading, as it was thought, the erstwhile privacy of the dream world. In the intervening years, other physiological changes have been shown to accompany rapid eye movements (abbreviation, REM) and low voltage brain waves. These include accelerated and more variable heart rate and breathing, relaxation of the head and neck muscles, and partial or complete erection of the penis. As a result of these physiological studies of sleep it is now customary to speak of two kinds of sleep. One kind is REM sleep which has already been described; the other kind is characterized by ocular quiescence, by more regular breathing and heart beat, by tension in head and neck muscles, by absence of penile erections, and by slower, higher voltage brain waves. This type of sleep is referred to as non-rapid eye movement sleep (abbreviation, NREM).

It was established by early investigations that an adult has four or five separate REM periods during a night of normal sleep. The first period appears about an hour after a person falls asleep, and thereafter they occur at intervals of approximately ninety minutes. The first REM period of the night is ordinarily very short and may even be skipped; the periods become longer as the night progresses. The final REM period of the night may last as long as an hour. REM periods constitute about 20 per cent of the sleep period in young adults. The percentage of REM sleep is considerably higher in infancy, and appears to be less in old age. REM sleep has been observed in a number of mammalian species which raises the perennial question, do animals dream? Unfortunately, an animal cannot be awakened and asked if it was dreaming. Undaunted by this insurmountable language barrier, however, one investigator performed the following ingenious experiment. Monkeys were trained while they were awake to avoid being shocked by pressing a bar whenever pictures were flashed on a screen. Later, when they were asleep, the monkeys spontaneously pressed the bar during REM periods but not during NREM periods. These findings suggest that the monkeys were responding to internal visual images; that is, to a dream.

It has become customary among some sleep and dream researchers to refer to REM sleep as dreaming sleep or simply as dreaming. This convention of taking the indicators for the process they are supposed to indicate—that is, of calling eye movements or brain waves dreaming—reflects an imprecision in the use of language which is uncharacteristic of scientific discourse. Not only does it tend to create misconceptions in the mind of the uninitiated reader but it also unconsciously persuades the investigator that he is studying something which in fact he is not. He begins to think and to write as though he were studying dreams when he is only studying the indicators of dreams. One may argue that the convention is justified by virtue of the fact that when a person is awakened during a REM period, he is more likely to say that he was dreaming and to be able to report a dream than when he is awakened during a NREM period. That is not the point, however. The point is that dreaming is *not* moving eyeballs, a particular pattern of brain waves, a tumescent penis, relaxed neck muscles, an irregularly beating heart, a varying rate of breathing, or any other measurable physiological condition. Dreaming is an experience that takes place during sleep. That is to say, dreaming is a psychological phenomenon and not a physiological one. This distinction between psychological and physiological is made for methodological purposes and not to assert a dualism of mind and body. Until such a time as dreaming can be televized the only way in which dreaming can be studied is by having a person report what he dreamed and then analyze the report using psychological methods. The EEG record cannot tell us *what* a person is dreaming or *why* he is dreaming it or *what* it means. It can only tell us *when* he is dreaming and it apparently does not tell that with complete accuracy. Recent findings strongly indicate that dreaming occurs during periods of sleep when the eyes are quiescent, that in fact it takes place at any time during the night from the onset of sleep to final awakening. These findings have raised the question of the definition of a dream since some of the experiences reported by people when they are awakened during NREM periods are labelled thinking by them rather than dreaming. Moreover, independent judges are able to distinguish reports obtained upon NREM awakenings from reports obtained upon REM awakenings. NREM reports are judged to be more plausible, less bizarre, less emotional, less visual, and more concerned with contemporary events. Despite these differences, bizarre, hallucinatory "dreams" are obtained from NREM awakenings and thinking-type "dreams" are obtained from REM awakenings, so that it is impermissible to declare that dreaming occurs exclusively during REM periods.

Although the objective indicators are not themselves dreams, they can serve a number of useful purposes in dream research. Under ordinary circumstances, the average person remembers a dream about every third morning, although there are wide individual differences in dream recall. A few people have never remembered a dream in their whole life; at the other extreme, there are those who remember several dreams every morning. By monitoring sleep with an EEG machine and awakening a person during each REM period, the yield for three nights would be from 10 to 15 dreams. Moreover, it is possible to see whether dreams obtained early in the night differ in any important respects from dreams obtained later in sleep. And it can be determined whether the dreams of the same night have a common theme, as Freud believed. The question of whether dreams collected during the night differ from dreams remembered spontaneously in the morning is one that can be answered with the new techniques.

With the indicators, one can introduce various stimulus conditions before or during sleep, then wake the person up during a REM period to see what effect, if any, the experimental condition had upon the dream. For example, in one investigation movies were shown to subjects before they went to sleep; in another proper names were spoken to them during REM periods. In general, this type of experiment bears out what similar studies prior to 1953 showed, namely, that the influence of introduced stimuli upon dreams is a minimal one. Drugs are also being administered to see what effects they have upon dreams.

Correlations between physiological variables and dream contents can be made more easily by monitoring sleep with the EEG machine. One can make parallel records of heart beat, blood pressure, breathing, and other physiological functions and compare these functions with the contents of reported dreams. Is the nightmare type of dream accompanied by a different physiological picture than a pleasant dream? Do characteristic physiological changes accompany an overt sex dream, and if so, do these same changes accompany symbolized sex dreams? The same question can be asked in regard to overt and symbolized dreams of aggression.

Something that everyone does, presumably including other mammalian species, and that does not have to be learned, would appear to have some importance, be it biological, psychological, or both. A number of writers on dreams have suggested that dreaming is a kind of safety valve by which tension that has accumulated during the day is discharged during the night so that the person awakens refreshed in mind as well as in body. Freud said, for example, that we fulfill or attempt to fulfill repressed wishes in our dreams. This is its psychological function. Its biological function, according to Freud, is to guard sleep. For one who has monitored sleep night after night, using the EEG machine, it often appears that the sleeping person when he approaches a REM period begins to struggle. He seems on the verge of waking up—and sometimes he does, at least momentarily—and then the eyes begin to move and presumably he is having a dream.

By diligently watching the objective indicators it is possible to deprive the sleeping person of dreams that occur during REM periods by awakening him at the beginning of each REM period. If the hypothesis that the majority of dreams occur during REM periods is correct—and it is still very much in dispute whether they do—then a person who is deprived of REM sleep should also be partially dream deprived. A number of such "dream deprivation" studies (they are actually REM deprivation studies) have been done and they all agree on one finding: when a person is allowed to sleep undisturbed after several nights of REM sleep deprivation, the percentage of REM sleep increases. The amount of increase and the number of nights that an increase in REM sleep continues is determined by the extent of the deprivation, at least up to a certain point. In other words, the person makes up lost REM time. Inasmuch as events other than dreaming take place during REM sleep it cannot be concluded that there is a need to dream. About the only thing one can say with certainty is that there is a need for REM sleep. There is also a need for NREM sleep as other investigations have shown.

There is not much agreement among various investigators as to other effects of REM sleep deprivation. The very first investigation indicated that the subjects became increasingly nervous and tense during waking life as the experiment proceeded. They displayed various kinds of bizarre behavior, and it was felt they might have become psychotic had the experiment been continued long enough. Later experiments have failed to support these findings in all respects. Some subjects did not seem to be affected to any great extent by being deprived of REM sleep over rather long periods of time. These results suggest that there are large individual differences in tolerance for REM sleep deprivation. When cats are deprived of REM sleep, which can be done by destroying a small area in the brain (brainstem nucleus pontis caudalis) they manifest bizarre behavior which becomes progressively more disturbed, culminating in manic delirium, exhaustion, and death. Are these effects due to deprivation of dreaming, deprivation of REM sleep, or deprivation of some concomitant feature of REM sleep that has not been identified, *e.g.,* a toxic condition in the brain? These are questions to which no final answers are now available.

In spite of our high regard for the new research with objective indicators

we believe that the dream can only be made to divulge its secrets by a con-
frontation with the dream itself. This is what Freud did when he applied
the technique of free association to the dream text. By having a patient
free associate to the components of a dream * the significance of the dream
was uncovered. This is also what we tried to do in the present book by
analyzing a series of dreams reported over a period of time by a person
without benefit of free association. The analyses reported in this book are
largely qualitative in nature. Since its original publication in 1953, our
efforts have been directed towards standardizing the analyses and making
them more quantitative. We have been joined in this undertaking by a
number of other investigators so that the literature of quantitative dream
studies is a rapidly expanding one. Our work in this direction has recently
been presented in a volume entitled THE CONTENT ANALYSIS OF
DREAMS, co-authored by R. L. Van de Castle. This book is primarily a
study in taxonomy, consisting as it does of a number of empirical and
theoretical scales for anayzing the contents of dreams, it also gives norms
for the various categories of dream contents, and suggests how the scoring
can be done to enable the investigator to feed his data into high speed
computers.

The present book makes use of short dream series, that is, series of 15
to 25 dreams gathered from a person over a period of several months.
In the last ten years, we have acquired a number of long dream series,
some running to seven and eight hundred dreams, and one of over
three thousand dreams. These long dream series were recorded over a
period of years; in one case, the dreams span a fifty year period. The
people from whom these dreams were acquired come from all walks of
life. Several are professional people, one is a writer, several were students,
two were mental patients at the time their dreams were being reported,
one is a cook, one a factory worker, and another an office worker. They
range in age from 18 to 80 and differ in race and nationality. Their motives
for keeping track of their dreams varied. Some did it primarily out of

---

* In order to avoid circumlocutions, the term dream is used to mean the
dream as reported. That is the only way in which a dream is known to
others than the dreamer, in any event. This does not involve us in the same
predicament that we have criticized others for, namely, calling eye movements dreaming. Words are not indicators as eye movements are. They are
denotative; that is, they describe the dream as recalled. How accurate this
description is cannot be determined.

scientific curiosity, some for reasons of self-help, a few because they were asked to, and one because he believed that his dreams would disclose the names of winning horses in future races.

When these long dream series were analyzed by means of standardized scales, the result that astonished us the most was the great amount of thematic consistency that prevailed in each series. Each person dreamed about much the same sort of thing from year to year even when there were radical changes in his waking life. We attribute this consistency to the unchanging character of the unconscious from which dreams are believed to come. Freud said that the unconscious is timeless, meaning by that that it is fully formed by the age of six and does not change thereafter. Dreams appear to be variations on a few basic infantile wishes and fears that have not been fulfilled or resolved. These are the root conflicts of human existence which are described in detail in the present volume.

Symbolism has continued to be a central interest of the writer and since 1953 I have elaborated some ideas concerning this important and neglected subject. *Out of the Dream Came the Faucet* is probably my most significant new contribution to the question of dream symbolism. In this paper, I argue that the man who invented the faucet did so because he wanted a better penis. Generally speaking, everything man invents, devises, or finds ready-made in the world represents an attempt to improve his body, particularly his genitals. Not only man's dreams but his waking behavior and the "culture" he creates as well are attempts to gratify infantile wishes or to defend against infantile fears. Even as an adult he still wants to be the omnipotent infant.

In another article, *The Birth of a Symbol,* the actual decomposition of a symbol into a referent so that they existed side by side in the dream is described for the first time to my knowledge.

Empirical studies of symbolism are rare because adequate methodology has not been devised. One method that appears promising consists of showing contingencies between the contents of dreams and free associations to these contents. Using this method, it was demonstrated that the male stranger in dreams symbolizes the father. Another application of the contingency method is to show contingencies in the contents of a series of dreams. An illustrative application of this method was made on a dream series in which anal symbols seemed to predominate. Associations beyond those expected by chance were found among such dream items as tunnel, rear, tight, dirty, explosion, vacant, brown, water, train, boat, church, odor, removed, and stone.

Another method of demonstrating that there are symbols in dreams is to make predictions as to what will be found in the dreams of contrasted groups, males versus females, for instance, when these predictions are based upon symbolic representations in dreams. Thus, Van de Castle and I hypothesized that there would be more castration anxiety in the dreams of males and more castration wish and penis envy in the dreams of females. Since castration and penis envy are rarely directly represented in dreams, it was necessary to establish criteria for their symbolic representation. These consisted of such items as injury to a part of the body, a defect in a personal possession, *e.g.,* a broken gun, and stealing an automobile from another person. The predictions were confirmed which indicated that the symbolic expressions were correctly designated.

Still another method we have employed for elucidating dream symbols is to look for their counterparts in slang. Such an investigation showed that virtually all of the categories of slang expressions for penis, vagina, and sexual intercourse are found in dreams.

Other topics that have continued to interest us are testing hypotheses drawn from Freudian psychology and the compilation of normative data on such dream contents as characters and social interactions.

I would like to take advantage of this introduction to a new edition of THE MEANING OF DREAMS to answer several criticisms that have been made of this book. The criticism that the analyses presented in it are qualitative rather than quantitative has been answered, it is to be hoped, by our recent preoccupation with quantifying content analysis.

Psychoanalytically-oriented critics have tended to be critical of anyone who limits his investigations to the "manifest" or reported dream. They maintain that the meaning of the dream resides in the free associations to the dream and not in the dream text itself. This criticism stems from the distinction Freud drew between manifest and latent content. By latent content, Freud meant the thoughts and wishes out of which the experienced dream is composed by the dream work. The dream work consists of a number of operations such as condensation, displacement, and symbolization. The manifest dream is decomposed into its constituent dream thoughts and wishes by having the dreamer free associate to the dream.

In answering this criticism, Van de Castle and I had this to say. "As a matter of fact, it could be said that there is no such thing as the latent content of a dream. A dream is a manifest experience, and what is latent lies outside the dream and in the verbal material that the dreamer reports when he is asked to free associate to features of the reported dream. How the psychoanalyst arrives at the 'true meaning' or interpretation of the dream from the verbalized associations is more of an art than a technique. This art may be of the utmost value in the therapeutic situation but being a private, subjective type of activity it is of no direct value for research. Indirectly, of course, it may provide a seedbed of ideas for research which may be carried out when objective methods for verbal analysis have been devised. *One can, of course, treat free associations as verbal material, which they are, and apply content analysis to them, just as one applies content analysis to reported dreams.* [Italics not in the original] The two records may then be analyzed for the presence of contingencies between them."

The assumption that reported dreams constitute valuable research material for enlarging our understanding of man will be tested finally in the crucible of investigatory activity. A number of investigators, including some research-oriented psychoanalysts, are studying reported dreams, and their findings, it seems to me, are significant contributions. The work of the late Dorothy Eggan on Navaho dreams, of Leon Saul and Edith Sheppard on psychosomatic patients, and of Aaron Beck and his associates on depressed patients exemplifies the usefulness of the reported dream.

In conclusion I would like to make some predictions of the directions in which I think dream research will go in the future. Monitoring sleep using the EEG machine is a technique that will continue to unlock many doors but it may also lead investigators up blind alleys. If we can judge from the past, the application of physiological methodology to psychological phenomena will not and probably cannot elucidate the psychological phenomena *per se.* EEG studies have already produced confusion regarding the definition of a dream and the nature of dreaming. It is to be expected that this confusion will expand rather than contract as more "physiologizing" is perpetrated on the dream. This is a purely methodological issue. The right methodology for one set of problems may be the wrong methodology for a different set of problems.

Psychological methodology for studying dreams will continue to improve. This improvement will consist not only of the validation of scales for the content analysis of dreams but also of the development of more sophisticated quantitative methods for treating content data. Theoretical models other than a Freudian one will be invoked to provide fruitful leads for the understanding of dreams. Richard Jones has made an adaptation of a developmental model devised by Erikson for use with dreams, and there are indications that Jungian theory can be applied quantitatively to dream reports.

Investigations of the relationship of dreams to waking life behavior are sorely needed. It is a sobering experience to discover, as I recently did, the enormity of the misjudgments that can be made in assessing a person's waking behavior from his dreams. It came about in this way. James T. Lester, Jr., the psychologist with the American Mount Everest Expedition, furnished me with dreams collected from the climbers and with coded personality sketches of the climbers that Lester had formulated based upon his daily observations of the men. In addition, I was supplied with assessments that the men had made of each other, as well as with data obtained from evaluations of the men by an independent organization prior to their leaving the United States. In general, my analyses of the men from their dreams agreed with those made by Lester, the men themselves, and the Institute of Personality Assessment and Research. There were two very bad misses, however. Two men whom I had rated as being the most popular climbers, the most mature psychologically, and the most effective leaders and morale builders of the Expedition turned out to be exactly the opposite in every respect. They were the least liked, the most immature, and had no leadership or morale building assets whatsoever. Further studies are needed to find out how general such discrepancies are and why they occur.

Cross-cultural studies of dreaming will soon be booming partly because cross-cultural investigations of all kinds are presently in fashion and partly because dreams are of concern to almost all peoples of the world except possibly for Western Europeans and Americans for whom dreaming is often taken to be an idle pastime hardly worthy of a serious man's attention. Those of us at the Dream Institute who are in touch with many dream collectors know the rapidly increasing accession of dreams from many parts of the world.

Systematic studies of children's dreams should reveal startling information about the inner life of the child. What little knowledge we have of children's dreams suggest that their dreams are much more complex and much more dreadful than has previously been thought.

Another promising research area is the comparison of dreams from persons afflicted with various psychosomatic disorders. Such studies would, I venture to guess, turn up some interesting correlations between dream content and somatic symptoms.

Finally, I believe that symbolism, not only symbolism in dreams but also symbolism in waking life, is on the verge of becoming an extremely fruitful research area. It is my guess that findings in this area will illuminate the infantile character of political, economic, religious, and military behavior.

These are only a few of the many directions that dream research can and probably will take. We can thank the observant eyes of Eugene Aserinsky and Nathaniel Kleitman in their Chicago laboratory for bringing about a renaissance in dream research.

I am indebted to an enormous number of people who have been my tutors, coworkers, and critics. These include students, colleagues, dream collectors, and those whom I know only through their writings. I wish to take this opportunity to thank all of them and at the same time to absolve them of all responsibility for the use that I have made of their ideas. Three people who have been closely associated with the activities of the Dream Institute and who have had the profoundest influence on my thinking in recent years are Bill Domhoff, Dick Jones, and Bob Van de Castle. I want to thank them especially for their friendly criticisms.

Calvin S. Hall
Director, Institute of Dream Research
Santa Cruz, California
March, 1966

Page xi. A good introduction to recent work on dreams for the general reader is *The Science of Dreams* by Edwin Diamond (Doubleday, Garden City, N. Y., 1962). It is also available in a paperback edition (McFadden, New York). An even more recent account is one published by the United States Department of Health, Education, and Welfare, *Current Research on Sleep and Dreams.* It may be ordered from the Superintendent of Documents, U. S. Government Printing Office, Washington, D. C. for 65 cents. Just published as this Introduction was being written is *Dreams and Dreaming* by Norman MacKenzie (Vanguard, New York, 1966). A sprightly journalistic account of the work being done in one sleep laboratory was published in the *New Yorker* magazine, September 18, 1965. Several review articles of EEG oriented studies have appeared in scientific books and journals: Frederick Snyder, The new biology of dreaming, *Archives of General Psychiatry,* 1963, Volume 8, pp. 381–391; William C. Dement, An essay on dreams: The role of physiology in understanding their nature, in *New Directions in Psychology II* (Holt, Rinehart, & Winston, New York, 1965); Charles Fisher, Psychoanalytic implications of recent research on sleep and dreaming, *Journal of the American Psychoanalytic Association,* 1965, Volume XIII, pp. 197–303; and Ernest L. Hartmann, The D-state, *New England Journal of Medicine,* 1965, Volume 273, pp. 30–35, 87–92.

Standard scientific works of recent vintage on sleep and dreams are Ian Oswald, *Sleeping and Waking* (Elsevier, Amsterdam, 1962); Nathaniel Kleitman, *Sleep and Wakefulness* (University of Chicago Press, Chicago, Ill., 1963); and Edward J. Murray, *Sleep, Dreams, and Arousal* (Appleton-Century-Crofts, New York, 1965). New books on dreams alone include Medard Boss, *The Analysis of Dreams* (Philosophical Library, New York, 1958); Walter Bonime, *The Clinical Use of Dreams* (Basic Books, New York, 1962); Richard M. Jones, *Ego Synthesis in Dreams* (Schenkman, Cambridge, Mass., 1962); Thomas M. French and Erika Fromm, *Dream Interpretation* (Basic Books, New York, 1964); and Calvin S. Hall and Robert L. Van de Castle, *The Content Analysis of Dreams* (Appleton-Century-Crofts, New York, 1966).

Page xii. The monkey experiment was performed by C. J. Vaughn at the University of Pittsburgh and is reported in his doctoral dissertation, "The development and use of an operant technique to provide evidence for visual imagery in the rhesus monkey under 'sensory deprivation' ."

Page xiii. The literature on NREM dreams is a growing one. See for example the following articles: David Foulkes, Theories of dream formation and recent studies of sleep consciousness, *Psychological Bulletin,* 1964, Volume 62, pp. 236–247, and Donald R. Goodenough, Helen B. Lewis, Arthur Shapiro, Leroy Jaret, and Irving Sleser, Dream reporting following abrupt and gradual awakenings from different types of sleep, *Journal of Personality and Social Psychology,* 1965, Volume 2, pp. 170–179.

Page xiv. For a comparison of early versus late dreams of the night see Bill Domhoff and Joe Kamiya, Problems in dream content study with objective indicators: III. Changes in dream content throughout the night, *Archives of General Psychiatry,* 1964, Volume 11, pp. 529–532.

Page xiv. Whether dreams of the same night have a common theme has been studied by a number of investigators. One of the most recent articles is Milton Kramer, Roy M. Whitman, Bill J. Baldridge, and Leonard M. Lansky, Patterns of dreaming: The interrelationship of the dreams of a night, *Journal of Nervous and Mental Disease,* 1964, Volume 139, pp. 426–439.

Page xiv. A comparison of dreams collected in the laboratory with dreams remembered at home in the morning has been made by Bill Domhoff and Joe Kamiya, Problems in dream content study with objective indicators: I. A Comparison of home and laboratory dream reports, *Archives of General Psychiatry,* 1964, Volume 11, pp. 519–524, and by Calvin S. Hall and R. L. Van de Castle (unpublished).

Page xiv. The effect of movies shown to persons prior to their going to sleep has been investigated by Herman A. Witkin and Helen B. Lewis, The relation of experimentally induced presleep experiences to dreams: a report on method and preliminary findings, *Journal of the American Psychoanalytic Association,* 1965, Volume XIII, pp. 819–849.

Page xiv. The influence of speaking proper names to a sleeping person on his dreams is reported by Ralph J. Berger, Experimental modification of dream content by meaningful verbal stimuli, *British Journal of Psychiatry,* 1963, Volume 109, pp. 722–740.

Page xv. The "dream deprivation" studies are reviewed by William Dement in his "Essay on Dreams" (See reference above).

Page xvi. The account of the analysis of a long dream series is by Madorah E. Smith and Calvin S. Hall, An investigation of regression in a long dream series, *Journal of Gerontology,* 1964, Volume 19, pp. 66–71.

Page xvii. The exact references for the papers relating to symbolism are as follows: Out of a dream came the faucet, *Psychoanalysis and the Psychoanalytic Review,* 1962, Volume 49, pp. 113–116; The birth of a symbol, in *Psychopompology: Studies in the Timeless Unconscious* by Bill Domhoff and Calvin S. Hall; Strangers in dreams: An empirical confirmation of the Oedipus complex, *Journal of Personality,* 1963, Volume 31, pp. 336–345; A pre-Freudian anal character, in *Psychopompology: Studies in the Timeless Unconscious* by Bill Domhoff and Calvin S. Hall; An empirical investigation of the castration complex in dreams (with Robert L. Van de Castle), *Journal of Personality,* 1965, Volume 33, pp. 20–29; and Slang and dream symbols, *The Psychoanalytic Review,* 1964, Volume 51, pp. 38–48.

Page xviii. The references for hypothesis testing in addition to those given above for symbols, and for normative material are as follows: A modest confirmation of Freud's theory of a distinction between the superego of men and women, *Journal of Abnormal and Social Psychology,* 1964, Volume 69, pp. 440–442; A ubiquitous sex difference in dreams (with Bill Domhoff), *Journal of Abnormal and Social Psychology,* 1963, Volume 66, pp. 278–280; Aggression in dreams (with Bill Domhoff), *International Journal of Social Psychiatry,* 1963, Volume 9, pp. 259–267; and Friendliness in dreams (with Bill Domhoff), *Journal of Social Psychology,* 1964, Volume 62, pp. 309–314.

Page xviii. This quotation is from page 20 of *The Content Analysis of Dreams.*

Page xix. An excellent discussion of cross-cultural studies of dreams is one by Dorothy Eggan in *Studying Personality Cross-culturally,* edited by Bert Kaplan (Harper & Row, New York, 1961). The work of Saul and Sheppard is reported in the following articles: Edith Sheppard and L. J. Saul, An approach to a systematic study of ego functions, *Psychoanalytic Quarterly,* 1958, Volume 27, pp. 237–245; Edith Sheppard, Systematic dream studies: clinical judgment and objective measurements of ego strength, *Comprehensive Psychiatry,* 1963, Volume 4, pp. 263–270; and Edith Sheppard and B. Karon, Systematic studies of dreams: relationship between the manifest dream and associations to the dream elements, *Comprehensive Psychiatry,* 1964, Volume 5, pp. 335–344. The work of Beck and his associates is reported in the following articles: A. T. Beck and M. S.

Hurvich, Psychological correlates of depression. I. Frequency of 'masochistic' dream content in a private practice sample, *Psychosomatic Medicine,* 1959, Volume 21, pp. 50–55; and A. T. Beck and C. H. Ward, Dreams of depressed patients: characteristic themes in manifest content. *Archives of General Psychiatry,* 1961, Volume 5, pp. 462–467.

Page xix. The reference to Jones is *Ego Synthesis in Dream* (Schenkman, Cambridge, Mass., 1962), and the application of Jungian theory to quantitative dream analysis is an article by F. Beyme, Archetypischer Traum (Todeshochzeit) und psychosomatische Symptom (weibliche Impotenz) im Lichte der Forschungen von J. J. Bachofen, C. G. Jung und Neumann, *Schweizer Archiv für Neurologie, Neurochirugie und Psychiatrie,* 1963–1964, Volumes 92–94, pp. 140–173, 100–136, 125–153.

Page xx. This study of the dreams of the Mt. Everest climbers has not been published but an account of Lester's activities as the Expedition psychologist will be found in his article, Men to match Mount Everest, *Naval Research Reviews,* December, 1964 and in James Ramsey Ullman, *Americans on Everest,* (J. B. Lippincott, New York, 1964).

1   What Dreams Are

THIS VOLUME is not just another book on dreams. It is not a history of what people have said about dreams from ancient times down to the present. It is not a rehash of modern dream theory as found in the writings of Freud, Jung, Stekel and other psychoanalysts. It is not a book based upon the dreams of abnormal people or patients undergoing treatment as so many books are. Nor is it a dream book which tells the reader how he can mechanically translate his dreams for the purpose of foretelling the future. An abundance of such books are already in print and another one would serve no useful purpose.

The present volume is unique because it contains an account of dreams which is based upon the study of thousands of dreams collected from hundreds of normal people. It represents the first attempt in the history of science to find out what normal people dream about and what their dreams mean in terms of their own personalities. It is a study of people as seen through their dreams. We subscribe wholeheartedly to Emerson's dictum that "a skillful man reads his dreams for his self-knowledge."

This book is unique in another respect. It describes a new method of interpreting dreams, one which we have called the dream series method. A dream series is a number of dreams dreamed by a single individual over a period of time. Instead of analyzing each dream separately, as is usually done in dream analysis, the dreams of a series are thought of as being a sequence of interrelated events like the chapters of a novel. Each dream contributes something to the total picture of the person as it is finally formulated. Moreover, interpretations of the dreams of a series provide a check upon one another so that we are less likely to get a one-sided view of the person than we would if we had only one dream to work on. The larger the sample of dreams collected from a person the more accurate and comprehensive the picture of the person becomes. We feel that the dream series method is an important innovation in the study of dreams and that its use as demonstrated throughout this book has enlarged our understanding of human personality.

In order to understand what dreams may contribute to our self-knowledge and to our knowledge of others, it is necessary to recognize that dreaming is a natural form of behavior exhibited by most people and to describe the common characteristics and properties of dreams. The following introduction is intended to open vistas for the reader which succeeding chapters will explore in greater detail.

A dream is a succession of images, predominantly visual in

quality, which are experienced during sleep. A dream commonly has one or more scenes, several characters in addition to the dreamer, and a sequence of actions and interactions usually involving the dreamer. It resembles a motion picture or dramatic production in which the dreamer is both a participant and an observer. Although a dream is a hallucination, since the events of a dream do not actually take place, the dreamer experiences it as though he were seeing something real. Scenes, people, objects and actions often seem just as real to the dreamer as they would if seen by him in waking life. Sometimes we even confuse a dream with an actual experience and ask ourselves, "Did it really happen or was it only a dream?" The apparent reality of a dream is also evidenced by the fact that we may wake up with pounding heart and rapid breathing or a scream on our lips because something frightened us in a dream. Talking and walking during sleep also confirm the idea that a dream is often experienced as though it were real.

The fact that a dream is a succession of mental pictures accounts for the finding that a dream occupies only a brief period of time, perhaps only a few seconds in many instances. A picture is very economical since it manages to say a great deal in a short space of time. As Turgenev, the great Russian novelist of the nineteenth century observed, "A picture may instantly present what a book could set forth only in a hundred pages."

The apparent reality of dream experiences is responsible for the ancient notion that dreams are actual experiences of the soul which has become detached from the body during sleep and roams heaven and earth. The dream according to this view is a record of the soul's nocturnal journey. This quaint notion gave rise to some equally quaint customs. For instance, it was thought to be dangerous to awaken a sleeping person suddenly since the soul might not have had time to get back into the body, in which event the person would die. There is a story told about a queen of Libya who sought payment from a young man after he confessed to having had sexual relations with her in a dream. The queen argued that since the man's soul had enjoyed itself carnally with her he should pay the usual price for such pleasure.

Although the idea of a wandering soul is not believed by most people today, there is a similar notion that dreams are real experiences which are produced by sounds, smells and lights, temperature changes, bodily positions, bladder pressure, stomach aches, muscular cramps, fever, and other external and internal forces acting upon the sleeping person. It cannot be denied that bodily states and external happenings do produce dreams. Everyone who dreams can recall a bladder dream or a muscular cramp dream or an alarm clock dream or one which can be traced to a specific condition. Experiments have been performed in the laboratory on sleeping persons which demonstrate that a bottle of perfume held under the nose, stroking or pinching a part of the body, depressing one side of the bed, or a cry for help are registered in dreams. Dreams have even been traced to the luminous patterns of dots and lines that occur naturally in the eye in the absence of external light.

The "stomach ache" theory of dreams or what Thomas Hobbes, the seventeenth-century philosopher, called "the distemper of inward parts" is a favorite explanation of dreams.

Hobbes illustrated this view in the following manner. During waking life, he says, the emotion of anger causes some part of the body to become overheated. When during sleep this same part of the body rises in temperature due to internal changes, the effect is to produce a dream in which the dreamer is angry. We all know of children who dream that they are going to the bathroom and awaken to find that the bed is wet, or adults who dream that they are having sexual relations and awaken to find they are having an orgasm. Kinsey in his comprehensive study of sexual behavior in the human male found that nocturnal emission dreams, commonly called "wet dreams," are very prevalent. It has been experimentally demonstrated that nightmares may be induced when respiration is interfered with. Dreams have even been traced to secretions of the endocrine glands.

The notion that dreams are produced by "the distemper of inward parts" found practical application in the early diagnosis of physical disorders from dreams. Dreams that result from incipient diseases are called *prodromic* dreams. "Prodromic" comes from a Greek word *prodromos* meaning a "forerunner," whence our English meaning, "a premonitory sign of disease." Aristotle and Hippocrates believed in prodromic dreams and even in modern times physicians have made use of dreams for diagnosing disorders. For example, dreams of being suffocated, of being crushed, or of flying are supposed to indicate that the person has the beginnings of a lung disease. Inasmuch as modern medical science has developed more accurate methods of early diagnosis dreams are rarely used by physicians today.

Although it cannot be denied that some dreams may contain material that is derived from happenings in the external or internal environment of the sleeping person, this explanation does not explain all dreams, or even most dreams. Nor does it account for the fact that the dream nearly always contains more material than that which can be traced directly to the stimulus. Moreover, the stimulus often appears in the dream, not in its true form, but in some distorted way. Let us examine the evidence for each of these objections to the theory that dreams are merely perceptions of things happening to the sleeping person.

Back in 1893 two well-trained experimental psychologists, a man and a woman, kept careful records of their dreams for a period of weeks, in order to see how many of them contained features that could be traced to some type of stimulation. In the 375 dreams recorded by them they could only find about 35 dreams in which such features occurred. Since they used an alarm clock to waken themselves in the middle of the night to record their dreams, it is surprising that the ringing of the alarm did not produce more dreams of this type. These findings are borne out by the writer's observation of his own dreams. Rarely do perceptions of external or internal events find representation in his dreams, and when they do the perceptual element is apt to be a minor part of the dream. In regard to this last point, it has been observed over and over again that so-called stimulus-produced dreams include more than the stimulus. Carefully performed experiments support this contention. For example, the following dream was reported following the utterance of the word "Help" in the ear of the sleeping person.

I was driving along the highway at home. Heard yelling and we stopped. A car was turned sideways in the road. I went down and saw the car was turned over on the side of the road. A man crawling out. Said he wasn't hurt. He told me someone was under the car. I helped turn the car over. There was a woman badly cut. We took her to the hospital.

This dream is in keeping with the experience of hearing a cry for help, but the details of driving along a highway, the overturned car, the badly cut woman and the unhurt man, and the trip to the hospital are all supplied by the dreamer.

Moreover, it has been demonstrated again and again that the stimulus, whether it be an alarm clock ringing, a car backfiring, a cold wind or a numb arm, is not experienced in a dream as it actually is but is distorted in some fashion. The ringing alarm is represented as church bells or the siren of a fire engine, the backfiring car is heard as a pistol shot or an earthquake, the cold wind is experienced as a trip by dogsled through the frozen north, and a numb arm is felt to be a snake curling itself around the dreamer's bosom. The same stimulus may be experienced in a variety of ways by different dreamers or by the same dreamer in different dreams. In one experiment, a wax candle was placed in the hand of the sleeping person on two different occasions. The first time he dreamed he was playing golf and the second time that he was trying to lift a bar in a physical training class.

If dreams cannot be explained adequately by things which are happening to the dreamer during sleep, how are they to be explained? I would explain them in this way. In the first place the images of a dream are projections of the mind. A projection is a representation of what is in the mind. For example, when a person makes up a story, he puts his thoughts and feelings into the story. It is said that the story represents or expresses his ideas. The artist when he paints a picture out of his imagination is projecting onto the canvas what is in his mind. On the other hand, if he paints a picture of a landscape while he is looking at the landscape, the resulting picture may be a faithful representation of the scene as it actually is, in which case the painting is not a projection. However, most artists do not paint scenes as they actually are. They change them to a greater or lesser degree. The greater the distortion of external reality, the more the artist is putting his own ideas and feelings into the picture.

Suppose a woman is walking along a deserted street at night and she is afraid that someone is going to jump out from the shadows and attack her. As she turns a corner, she screams and faints, because she *thinks* she sees a man hiding behind a telephone post ready to spring upon her, when in fact "the man" is a mailbox partly hidden by the pole. In this case, the woman has projected her fear upon a neutral object in the environment. Her terror of being attacked by a man makes her see a man instead of a mailbox.

It is helpful to distinguish between two kinds of projections. One kind consists of distorting objective reality. Projections of this type are called illusions or delusions. The mailbox seen as a man is an illusion because there was actually something in the environment for the woman to see but she misinterpreted it. An illusion is a faulty interpretation of an object. It is a mistaken perception, in which the mistake is caused by the person's mental state. A delusion is a mistaken judgment or belief. A person believes something to be true when it is actually false. Delusions are often caused by what is called "wishful thinking." A person wants something to be true so badly that he convinces himself that it is true. He reads his own wishes into the world and makes the world conform to his wishes.

A second kind of projection is one in which the person makes up something out of whole cloth and treats it as though it really existed. There is nothing in the external world at all, but he imagines there is. If the woman walking down the lonely street had seen a man and there was nothing there to support such a notion, no mailbox, post, shadow or anything else, then the seeing of a man would have been a hallucination instead of an illusion. A hallucination is the perception of an object without external cause.

Now dreams, except for those few which can be traced to the perception of an actual event, belong to the second kind of projection. Dreams are purely and simply hallucinations. We dream of two men fighting, one kills the other then runs home and hides, or we dream of walking down the aisle to the altar and being married to some person. Obviously these events are not really taking place. They are the hallucinations of a sleeping person.

Because dreams are hallucinations, should we therefore dismiss them as mere derangements of the mind unworthy of serious study and contemplation? If we did this to dreams then we would have to dismiss all of the great works of art, of literature, and of music, everything in fact that has been created out of the mind of man. For dreams, too, are creative expressions of the human mind. They are the portals through which we can view the workings of the mind. It is for this reason, and this reason alone, that dreams merit our serious attention.

Let us see just how dreams are formed. During sleep the

mind continues to function. The sleeping person is capable of thinking. Now thinking, whether it occurs in sleep or in the waking state, is one and the same process. Thinking consists of forming conceptions or ideas. A conception is an item of knowledge or a judgment which the person thinks is true although it may not be. He may conceive of the earth as being round or flat, of the sun moving around the earth or the earth around the sun, or of men being brighter than women or women brighter than men. The mind is engaged continually in forming ideas. A person may share his ideas with others by expressing them. The usual mode of expression in waking life is language, although other means, such as numbers, pictures, gestures and movements, music and three-dimensional forms are also used to convey ideas. The expression of an idea means to embody the idea in a form that can be perceived by an audience. Words when spoken can be heard or when written can be seen, and thus they are capable of making an impression upon the listener or the reader.

Dreams like language embody a person's thoughts. The language of a dream consists of pictures which are the concrete perceptible representations of the mind's ideas. A conception is invisible. When it is transformed into a dream image, it becomes visible. In short, the images of our dreams are pictures of our conceptions. We study dreams in order to find out what people are thinking about during sleep.

One major difference between a dream and the spoken or written word is that a dream has only the dreamer as its audience while the spoken or written word may reach thousands or even millions of people. It would be wonderful if one could televise the sleeping mind and broadcast dreams as one does

soap operas and mystery stories. One might be surprised to find
that dreams have much in common with the fantasies that are
dreamed up by television writers and producers!

The fact that the dreamer alone experiences his dream means
that dreams cannot be the direct object of study except by the
dreamer himself. In order for dreams to be studied objectively
it is necessary for the dreamer to tell us his dreams or have him
write them down. Any study of dreams is really a study of
dream narratives which are recalled and communicated by people when they awaken. It is fruitless to ask how much the dream
narrative resembles the original dream because the original
dream cannot be transcribed.

What kinds of conceptions are expressed by dreams? From
our study of thousands of dreams, we know that they are relatively silent about certain kinds of conceptions and relatively
vocal about others. Dreams contain few ideas of a political or
economic nature. They have little or nothing to say about current events in the world of affairs. I was collecting dreams daily
from students during the last days of the war with Japan when
the first atomic bomb was exploded, yet this dramatic event did
not register in a single dream. Presidential elections, declara-
tions of war, the diplomatic struggles of great powers, major
athletic contests, all of the happenings that appear in news-
papers and become the major topics of conversation among
people are pretty largely ignored in dreams. Businessmen ordinarily do not dream about their business affairs, factory workers do not dream about their jobs, artists do not dream about
painting, students do not dream about studying, and housewives
do not dream about household activities.

What then is there left to dream about? There is the whole

world of the personal, the intimate, the emotional and the con-
flictful, and it is this world of ideas out of which dreams are
formed. A dream is a personal document, a letter to oneself.
It is not a newspaper story or a magazine article.

In the first place dreams reveal what we really think of ourselves when the mask of waking life is removed. There we are
in our dreams acting out our system of self-conceptions. This
system may be a simple one, in which case the dreamer plays the
same part night after night, as exemplified by a young man
who saw himself in one dream after another as a personage of
great importance brought down to defeat after vigorous combat with a superior adversary. His dreams were an admission
to himself that no matter how strong he might become he would
always be humbled by someone stronger. Or the system of self-
conceptions may be a complex one in which case the roles played
by the dreamer in his dreams will be many and varied. If a
person should take a hundred of his dreams and observe in
each one the part he plays, he could then write an essay on the
subject "What I Really Think of Myself."

Of what importance are these self-conceptions? They are
important because what a person thinks about himself has a
great influence upon how he behaves. If a person thinks he is a
failure the chances are that he will try to live up to this image
of himself and be a failure. If he thinks that he is a moral repro-
bate, his life will be suffused with feelings of guilt and shame,
even though he may never have done anything in the eyes of
the world to justify such feelings. If one is convinced that he is
inadequate and inferior, he will have a difficult time meeting
the vicissitudes of life successfully. Probably in no other way

can we gain such candid and accurate information about a person's conception of himself as we can by a study of his dreams.

Dreams also reveal how the dreamer conceives of other people. What he thinks of his mother and father, his brothers and sisters, his spouse and children and diverse other people is embodied in the roles these various persons assume in his dreams. If a dreamer conceives of his father as a stern, demanding, autocratic person, the father is given a dream part in keeping with this conception. If a wife thinks her husband is a weak, impotent person incapable of satisfying her intimate needs, she will convey this picture of him in her dreams no matter what she may say she thinks of him in waking life. Dreams cut through the pretensions and deceits of waking life and lay bare the true feelings we have of people. If a woman sees men as threatening she will dream of men chasing and attacking her. Similarly if a young man is afraid of older men and what they might do to him he will dream of being attacked or punished by them. Like self-conceptions, our conceptions of other people may be simple or complex. For example, one may have formulated a rather complex system of ideas about one's father or mother. Some of these ideas may even be contradictory, as when a father is portrayed as both a friend and an enemy in one's dreams. Ideas may be contradictory because the laws of logic do not apply to our personal conceptions. If a system of thought regarding a person is complex, this complexity will be portrayed in dreams by a diversity of roles played by that person.

A word of caution should be mentioned at this point. The conceptions appearing in dreams should not be taken as dependable guides to objective reality. What one conceives to be true and what is actually true do not always coincide. A person may conceive of his mother as a grasping, selfish, conceited woman when, as judged by impartial observers, his mother does not possess these traits at all and may in fact be just the opposite in character. Dreams should never be read for the purpose of constructing a picture of objective reality. They should be studied for the sole purpose of learning about subjective reality, by which is meant those conceptions which reside in a person's mind irrespective of their truth or falsity.

Dreams also yield information about the dreamer's conceptions of the world. By the world is meant the environment in its totality, that which surrounds a person. This world outside may be viewed as benign, hostile, turbulent, sorrowful, lonely, degraded and in numerous other ways. In dreams, these conceptions of the world are often conveyed by the character of the dream setting. If a dreamer feels that the world is cold and bleak, he may materialize this conception by having the dream take place on a rocky coast in freezing weather. If he thinks that the world is full of turmoil and agitation, he will dream of thunderstorms, raging seas, battles, milling crowds and traffic jams. A feeling that the world is benign and peaceful can be scenically represented in dreams by serene natural settings.

During sleep, it is not uncommon for impulses that are kept in check during waking life to express themselves in dreams. Noting this fact, Freud came to the conclusion that the satisfaction of impulses or as he called it the fulfillment of wishes was the main reason for dreaming. It can hardly be denied that many dreams are motivated by sex and aggression, or if the dreamer has been without food and water for a long time, by hunger and thirst. It is hardly necessary, however, to consult dreams in order to discover that man seeks gratification of his urges. What dreams can tell us with greater profit to an understanding of ourselves and others is how the dreamer conceives of his impulses. Does he, for example, consider sex a wicked, depraved force? If so, his sex dreams will reflect this conception. Or does he have a purely mechanical conception of sex as something that can be turned on and off like a faucet. If so, he may have a dream like the following one reported by a young man.

I got out of bed and went into the bathroom and attempted to turn on the water faucet. I turned and turned but no water came out. I then decided to call a plumber. Soon afterward the door opened and an individual dressed in coveralls approached me. Upon closer examination I discovered the plumber was a female. I scoffed at the idea of a lady plumber, but unruffled she went to the basin, turned the faucet, and water immediately flowed. At this point, I awoke having a nocturnal emission.

Impulse dreams not only reveal the dreamer's conception of his impulses, but they also tell us something about the nature of the object by which he hopes to gratify his impulse. People who are sexually attracted to members of their own sex usually dream about having homosexual relations. A person who has feelings of enmity toward older men will find an outlet for these feelings in his dreams. Generally speaking, we can learn whom we think are our lovers and our enemies by studying our dreams.

Gratification of impulses does not always proceed smoothly. Obstacles are encountered and detours are necessary. The nature of these obstacles and the kinds of detours made are expressed in dreams. The principal obstacle is the dreamer's own conscience. Conscience is a network of conceptions of right and wrong, of sanctions and prohibitions. Prohibitions are represented in dreams by walls, curbs, and locked doors, by acts of restraint such as applying the brakes of a car, or by the appearance of a policeman who threatens to arrest the dreamer. Whether the dreamer can evade the prohibition and if so, how he does it is portrayed in dreams. One young man who has a fairly strong prohibition against satisfying himself sexually dreamed that he was seduced by a woman. Although his conscience would not permit him to take the initiative, the prohibition did not apply when he was cast in the role of the passive victim of a sexually aggressive woman. Our dreams are filled with alibis for doing things which our conscience tells us is wrong. We are hypocrites even in our dreams.

Many dreams are unpleasant, even terrifying as in the case of nightmares. The dreamer is being chased by a man with a knife, a burglar is entering his room, a lion is about to spring on him, the house is on fire, he is drowning or he is arrested and put in prison. These are all punishment dreams. For what reason is the dreamer being punished? Because he has violated one of the commandments of his conscience. He has rebelled against authority, or he has gratified a forbidden wish, or he has committed a misdeed. The nightmare is the price he pays for doing something wrong. Such dreams provide us with information about the dreamer's conceptions of the penalties that will be inflicted upon him should he disregard his conscience and yield to temptation.

Dreams, then, reveal how the dreamer conceives of his impulses, how and with whom he would like to satisfy them, what prohibitions stand in the way of wish-fulfillment, how he tries to get around these prohibitions and what penalties he will suffer if he ignores the voice of conscience.

The most important information provided by dreams has yet to be mentioned, namely, information about the dreamer's problems and conflicts. Everyone has problems and everyone tries to do something about them. Unfortunately, though, we are rarely aware of the true nature of our conflicts. Lacking such knowledge, we are unable to solve our problems. Dreams, however, have a way of cutting through the pretensions and delusions of waking life and bringing the dreamer face to face with his real problems. Caught in the web of conflict, his dreams are a record of the struggles he makes to free himself. This, above all, is what dreams are, an authentic record of a mind made anxious by conflict.

Although it has been said that dreams are relatively mute about matters that concern the person during waking life, this does not mean that the thoughts of sleep are entirely separate and distinct from the thoughts of waking life. It has been fairly well established that some aspects of the dream are usually connected with events of the previous day or immediate past. One dreams about a person that he has not seen for many years, and the dreamer, on awakening, wonders why this person should emerge from the remote past to play a part in his dream. It will ordinarily be found that something occurred during the previous day to remind one of the forgotten person. The occurrence may have been only a fleeting one so that it is forgotten almost as soon as it is remembered, but still the thought persists undercover to emerge that night in a dream. The wakeful mind is customarily preoccupied with the external world and does not pay much attention to inner promptings. Just the opposite is the case during sleep. The mind is preoccupied with undercover material and does not pay much attention to the external world. Some of the undercover material consists of events which happened during the day and were repressed.

We should like to close this chapter by showing how the foregoing ideas may be utilized in analyzing a dream. As we shall explain later, our method of dream interpretation consists of analyzing a series of dreams collected from a person rather than single dreams as is customary in most systems of dream interpretation. We are presenting the following dream secured from a young man to illustrate the material presented in this chapter.

I was at the blackboard in a schoolroom doing a trig problem, but I was having trouble with it because I could not remember the valence of nitrogen. I was about to give up on it when a girl came up to me, and asked if I would like to dance.

The music was good but very erratic, being very fast one instant, and very slow the next; however, we were always exactly in step. She was an excellent dancer. When the music stopped, we were both in the school shower but we still had our clothes on. I wanted to take hers off and make love to her, but I had never done anything like that before, so we just laughed and splashed water.

Then I was outside the school. It was night and lights shone in all the windows silhouetting a wild orgy of a party. I felt very lonely. I wanted to go inside, but something seemed to hold me back. I heard chimes ringing in the church.

In the opening scene, we see the dreamer hard at work on a mathematics problem with which he is having difficulty. His

self-conception is one of an industrious student engaged in a
purely intellectual task for which he does not have the necessary
knowledge. A girl appears and invites him to dance. By so doing,
he casts the girl in the role of a temptress and himself as her
willing victim. At her bidding, he deserts the hardships of intellectual activity for the pleasures of sensuality. Their sensuality
stops short of complete fulfillment because he cannot conceive
of himself as consummating the sexual act. The scene changes
in line with a new conception which comes into the dreamer's
mind. He now sees himself as a lonely outsider looking in on a
wild orgy. He would like to go in and join the fun but he is held
back by some force. The church bells, embodying as they do
ideas of virtue and morality, indicate that the unknown force is
a prohibition issuing from his conscience.

This dream, then, expresses two conflicting conceptions in
the mind of the dreamer, one in which the young man sees
himself as a moral, hardworking, intellectual person, the other
in which he sees himself as a sensual being. These opposing
ideas inhibit one another, so that he cannot maintain a consistent
conception of himself as being either moral or sensual. When
he is doing something that he considers to be right, he is dis-
tracted by sexual thoughts; when he is doing something that he
considers to be wrong, he is interrupted by ideas of morality.
He is unable to play either role successfully since he can neither
solve the intellectual task nor fulfill his sexual wish. This dream
is reminiscent of Tannhäuser's predicament as portrayed in
Wagner's opera. Tannhäuser, like our young dreamer, was
caught between the opposing forces of carnal sexuality and
moral virtue. Like our dreamer, the sound of church bells moved

Tannhäuser to renounce the pagan excesses of the court of Venus.

Speaking of Tannhäuser reminds us that there is no theme of mythology or literature which fails to be represented in the dreams of people living today. Had we the time we could show that the plots of Greek tragedy and those of Shakespeare are met with over and over again in dreams. Every man is his own playwright when he is asleep.

However, we must move on to other matters, the first of which will be to describe some common features of the contents of dreams.

2   What We Dream About

ALTHOUGH DREAMS have been the object of study and speculation for centuries and hundreds of books have been written about them no one has bothered to make a systematic analysis of what people dream about. A census of dreams has never been taken. It is said that dreams are bizarre and grotesque, and that they do not resemble the contents of the waking mind. Is this notion correct? The only way to find out is to examine a large number of dreams of normal people and make a classification of what one finds. This is what we have done. We have collected and read thousands of dreams to see what they are about and we now propose to divulge our findings.

Our first method of classification is a fourfold one, consisting of settings, characters, actions and emotions. These four features were chosen because most dreams contain all four and because it is fairly simple to break down any dream into these components. Moreover, as we shall show, these four aspects of a dream shed considerable light on the personality of the dreamer. We turn first to consider settings.

DREAM SETTINGS

A dream like a play nearly always has a setting. The setting may be one that is strange and unfamiliar to the dreamer, or it may be one that he recognizes in a vague and uncertain way without feeling quite at home in it. Other settings are taken from the dreamer's everyday life and appear in his dreams as faithful and realistic reproductions of familiar scenes. In a few dreams, about five in every hundred, the dreamer is not aware of the setting; in others, there is little else save scenery, as in the following dream of a young man.

I was standing on a cliff near the edge. As I look down I see huge blocks of stone and the sea pounding against them and churning itself into white, foamy and sparkling particles. As I gaze out calmly across the blue water, I can see the setting sun sink like a blazing ball of fire and it creates a golden path across the waters to my feet. The sky is light blue and very light on the horizon. Yet at the same time I feel as though there is a bright noonday sun shining down on me. I am standing on grass and it feels like a thick carpet beneath my feet, very soft and comforting. On the whole, the water is very blue and sometimes almost black or a deep purple violet.

In this pretty dream, there is no action, no people other than the dreamer, no strong emotion—just scenery.

In about fifteen out of every hundred dreams the dreamer is in a conveyance, the most frequent kind being an automobile, and to a lesser degree, airplanes, boats and streetcars. The significance of conveyance settings is that the dreamer is going somewhere, he is on the move, he is in motion. Movement represents such ideas as ambition, progress and achievement, breaking family ties, fleeing from something or dying. Automobiles, trains, boats and airplanes are instruments of power, and as such can stand for the vital energy of one's impulses, particularly the sex impulse. We use the language of conveyances when we speak of the "transports of love." In days gone by, the horse was a favorite embodiment of sexual energy in dreams, but the automobile and airplane have been displacing it as a symbol of virility in recent years.

Whether the dreamer is driving an automobile, steering a ship or piloting an airplane or whether he is merely a passenger in a conveyance signifies something about the dreamer's conception of himself. As a passenger, who is transported somewhere and who has little to say about the route, the destination or the way in which the vehicle is being driven, the dreamer is playing the part of a passive person who is dependent upon others. As the driver, he expresses a self-image of independence and mastery. An example of a dream which contains both of these conceptions is the following one reported by a young woman.

I dreamed that my father and I were in an old Chevrolet. I was driving but I could not seem to make the car go up a very steep hill, so my father took the wheel.

This dreamer is attempting to view herself as a person of independence but as the going gets rough she reverts to a role of dependence upon her father.

The manner in which the driver controls the car may also be revealing. If the driver loses control of it, hits another vehicle or pedestrian, goes over a cliff, breaks through the guard rail of a bridge, crashes a red light or plunges down a steep hill, this means that he sees himself being overwhelmed by uncontrollable impulses. If he avoids having an accident by a display of skill, this means that he has brought the impulse under control.

A setting closely allied to conveyances is one in which the dreamer is on or walking along a street or road. About ten out of every hundred dreams have this type of setting. They do not appear to have the significance that conveyance dreams do except for those in which the dreamer is crossing a bridge. This is rather an elegant symbol of a transition in one's life, a passing from youth to adulthood, from middle age to old age, or from life to death.

Dreamers spend quite a bit of their time in recreational settings, at dances and parties, on the beach and in swimming, watching sports events and visiting amusement parks. These settings are frankly sensual in character, involving as they do pleasure and fun. About one out of every ten dreams is of this type. In contrast, places where people work such as offices, factories, and stores rarely appear in dreams, which implies that dreams are oriented more toward pleasure than work.

Houses or rooms in houses are by far the most popular type of dream locale. One out of every three dreams occurs in a dwelling, although usually it is not the dreamer's own house.

Among the specific places in a house where dreams occur, the living room is the most popular, followed by bedroom, kitchen, stairway, basement, bathroom, dining room and hall in that order. The particular room chosen may have a special symbolic significance. A basement for example, is a place where *base* deeds are committed or represents *base* unconscious impulses. Both of these features can be found in the following dream reported by a middle-aged woman.

The dream took place in the basement. I was surrounded by my immediate family, consisting of my husband, son and daughter, and friends. The scene which had been friendly was interrupted by a young man I did not recognize. He revealed a gun in an obvious intent to kill one of my close friends (male). My husband engaged in a fist fight with the intruder, who was knocked unconscious. My husband and son carried the man into the next room, and then locked the door, instructing me to call the police.

The base intention of the intruder is quite clear; what may not be so clear is that the dreamer herself has summoned the young man with a gun into the dream in order to do away with one of her friends. In other words, the dreamer harbors a hostile feeling against this friend which she forces out of her thoughts by the expedient of having her husband knock out the intruder. The locking of the door and the calling of the police support this interpretation since the locked door stands for the setting up of a barrier against the dreamer's criminal urge while the calling of the police represents the voice of conscience which arrests her shameful wish.

Rural and out-of-doors settings are fairly common, one in ten dreams having such a location. They are more common in the dreams of men than of women. In fact, if we divide dream settings into two classes, inside a building versus outside, women have more of the former and men more of the latter. This finding is consistent with the belief that men find more satisfaction in freedom from confinement whereas women prefer the security of enclosed places.

Among the miscellany of dream locales, a few are deserving of comment not because they appear frequently in dreams but because of their symbolic significance. Bars and restaurants, for example, are places where people satisfy their oral needs, that is, drinking and eating. Interestingly enough, bars are more common in men's dreams while restaurants are more common in women's dreams. This suggests that men have a greater need to take in liquids whereas women have a greater need to take in solid food. Since one starts life on a liquid diet, dreams of drinking are more infantile than dreams of eating.

Prison dreams express two basic conceptions, confinement and punishment. The first attitude is portrayed in the following dream reported by a young man.

My dream began in a prison or what resembled one. The only barriers to escape were some iron railings which surrounded the enclosure. Suddenly without any warning, a section of the iron railing had disappeared and many people were seen running through the opening to the world outside. I saw my chance and ran through the opening and headed for the open country that surrounded the prison. I had a feeling of intense relief at having escaped from something which was not defined in the dream. At the same time I was disturbed by the fact that someone might see me escape and return me to the prison. My dream ended as I was running away from the prison.

What this young men is saying in this dream, and what he says in other dreams reported by him, is that he views his life as a prison from which he is trying to escape, but without much real conviction that he will be successful. Being arrested and thrown in jail is a straightforward self-punishment dream. The dreamer is punishing himself for having transgressed his moral code.

Battlefields are appropriate sites for dreams of aggression while a church provides an appropriate background for conceptions of goodness.

When one reflects on the character of dream settings as found in the dreams of normal people, one is astonished to find that they are really quite commonplace and ordinary. Dreams occur in prosaic and familiar surroundings—a living room, an automobile, a street, a grocery store, a beach or a restaurant. Exotic and strange locales are few and far between.

Usually the dreamer recognizes the surroundings and knows where he is, although sometimes he feels that there is something not quite right about the setting. The furniture is changed about or the arrangement of rooms is different from what it actually is. In these cases, the setting probably represents a combination of several places. The house that is not quite right may be a composite of several houses in which the dreamer has been or lived. It is similar to a dream character who is a composite picture of several people. Sometimes a dream setting will be one that the dreamer knew early in life and which he has since forgotten.

Although dream settings are usually conventional and familiar, they are not completely representative of the places in which people spend their time during waking life. Taking into consideration the amount of time people spend working, the scarcity of work settings in dreams is distinctly out of line. On the other hand, conveyance and recreational settings have a higher incidence in dreams than they do in waking life.

One last word about settings. Just as the setting for a theatrical performance often helps to clarify the meaning of the play, so the location of the dream may aid in understanding its meaning. However, one should not detach the setting from the total context in analyzing a dream and say "this setting always means this about the dreamer." Sometimes a setting conveys one idea, sometimes another. The general rule of dream interpretation applies here as elsewhere, that the meaning assigned to a feature of a dream should fit in with the meaning assigned to all other parts of the dream.

DREAM CHARACTERS

A dream also has a cast. First, there is the dreamer himself. His role may be a minor one, hardly more than that of a spectator, or he may be the hero of the piece. In about fifteen out of every hundred dreams, the dreamer is the sole character. In the other eighty-five dreams, there are, on the average, two characters in addition to the dreamer. Although a trio of dream actors is typical, there is a good deal of variation. Some dreams may be as thickly populated as an elaborate extravaganza.

Who are these persons of the dream and why do they come into our dreams? We have made an actual count of dream characters, classified as to age, sex and relationship to the dreamer. These are our findings based upon the analysis of thousands of dreams.

Members of the dreamer's family constitute a fairly high percentage of dream characters. For younger dreamers, those in their late teens and early twenties, mother and father are dreamed about more often than any other family members while among middle-aged dreamers the dreamer's mate and his children play important roles. Why should we dream about our family? We believe that the people who enter our dreams are ones with whom we are emotionally involved. The emotion may be one of love, fear or anger, or a mixture of these feelings. For young people who are not married and who do not have children, the most significant members of the family and the ones with whom they are emotionally involved are their parents. Young people are trying to break family ties and assert their independence yet they are apprehensive about leaving the security of home for the hazards of the world. Moreover, they often feel guilty about deserting their parents. On the other hand, older dreamers having resolved these particular conflicts find themselves involved with their husbands or wives and with their children. It is rather ironical that while children are dreaming about parents, parents are dreaming about children, and while husbands are dreaming about wives, wives are dreaming about husbands. It might be said that if a person wants to know who is dreaming about him, he will find the answer by consulting his own dreams. The people in his dreams are likely to be those who are dreaming about him.

Friends and acquaintances constitute another large class of dream characters. As might be expected, these characters are mostly of the same age as the dreamer. It is interesting that men dream more often about male friends and acquaintances than they do about females, while women dream about equally of both sexes. This is really a large and significant difference. Why should it be true? We believe that the same explanation used to account for the differences among family members holds here. For men, relations with other men are more unsettled than relations with women. Women, on the other hand, have about an equal amount of emotional conflict with members of both sexes.

About four out of every ten characters in our dreams are strangers. Strangers represent the unknown, the ambiguous and the uncertain. Strangeness both frightens and fascinates. Sometimes a stranger in our dreams stands for an alien part of our own personality which we are reluctant to acknowledge as belonging to us. Sometimes a stranger personifies an aspect of an individual we know. For example, a woman dreams about being attacked by an unfamiliar man. The man may personify one of the conceptions she has of her boy friend, brother, husband or father, a conception that he is to be feared because she imagines he wants to harm her. She may not be aware of this conception, but it comes out in her dream nevertheless.

We rarely dream about prominent people, people we read about in the paper, hear over the radio or see in the movies. This fits in with our contention that dreams have very little to do with the world of current events. For all of our apparent concern about the world of public affairs, this concern does not go very deep nor it is emotionally relevant for us.

It should be remembered that the dreamer is the author of his dream and that it is he and he alone who determines who shall be invited into his dream. He invites those people for whom he has mixed feelings of affection and antagonism. They are people about whom he has divergent conceptions and with whom he has not achieved a stable relationship. They are the focal points of unresolved tension. When the tension abates, the appearance of the person in one's dreams diminishes, when the tension increases his entrances are more numerous. Those people toward whom the dreamer feels both love and hate or fear and hate occupy the center of the dream stage. Putting it in another way it can be said that we do not dream about people with whom we have achieved a stable and satisfying relationship. A husband and wife, for example, will not dream about one another if they have unmixed feelings of affection for each other. Nor will a person dream about someone toward whom he feels neutral.

You may ask, "What about those people who come into our dreams and who mean very little to us in waking life? Why did I dream about the butcher the other night, and a casual acquaintance whom I haven't seen or thought about for years the night before? Surely I am not emotionally involved with these people." These people come into our dreams either because they stand for some significant aspect of our life or because they represent a feature of a person with whom we are involved or because they are associated with some past conflict that is reasserting itself in our present life or because they symbolize some trait within ourselves. The corner butcher may represent an aggressive tendency in ourselves or someone else and the casual acquaintance of years ago may have some connection with a revived tension of the past.

In order to illustrate how much information about the dreamer can be secured from paying attention to the people who enter his dreams, we have selected two series of dreams from our large collection. The first series was collected from a young man whom we shall call Harry. Harry, who is unmarried, dreams mostly about members of his family. His mother or a middeaged woman resembling his mother appears in seven dreams. In two of these dreams his mother is angry with him and in one he is angry with her. In two dreams his mother makes him feel guilty about a sexual transgression, and in another the dreamer feels guilty because he is leaving his mother. In the seventh dream the young man protects his mother from harm. Anger, guilt and affection are emotions that the mother arouses in this dreamer.

Harry's father or a man like his father appears in six dreams. In one his father is angry with the dreamer and in another the dreamer is angry with his father. In two dreams his father is attempting to encourage his son to overcome an obstacle and in two dreamer and father are having a good time together. Although his relations with his father seem to be better than those with his mother, there is still a residue of hostility in Harry's mind which prevents him from having an uncomplicated relationship with his father.

Harry's brothers, of whom he has several, are given parts in seven dreams. In four of these dreams, something bad happens to a brother. An older woman tries to push his brother into the path of a passing automobile, his brother is electrocuted despite the dreamer's efforts to rescue him, his brother cuts his own finger and the dreamer is pleased by this injury, and the dreamer plays mean pranks on his brother. In two dreams Harry and his brothers are having a good time together and in a third he is being protective toward one of his brothers. The dreamer has mixed feelings about his brothers just as he has about his mother and father. For Harry, the seat of his conflict rests in the family circle.

John, our second exhibit, never dreams about his family. This young married man dreams mostly about his wife and other women of his age. The nature of his conflict is that he is tempted to be unfaithful to his wife while his conscience tells him that this would be wrong. In five dreams he has or attempts sexual relations with other women. That he has a fairly strong resistance against being unfaithful is indicated by the fact that in several of these dreams he arranges to have the girl reject him. In one dream John is at a party with his wife when he sees an old girl friend to whom his wife objects. He avoids meeting her in order not to offend his wife, although he would like to talk with the girl. In another dream his wife and an old girl friend of John's are quarreling. John tries to break it up but he does not succeed. This quarrel reflects John's conflict. His love for his wife is quarreling with his desire for an affair with another woman.

That John wants sexual gratification outside of marriage and yet feels ashamed of himself for having this desire is supported by three dreams in which he is being criticized by other people. In one dream he is being talked about, in a second he is accused of ruining a stage production, and in a third a crowd of men and women are showing their disgust for him for being dirty.

John's conflict is quite different from the one portrayed in Harry's dreams, yet in both cases, the conflict determines what characters will be invited into the dreams.

We can sum up this section on dream characters in a single statement. We dream about people who are associated in some way with our personal conflicts.

DREAM ACTIONS

What does a dreamer do in his dreams? An analysis of hundreds of dreams gives the following answer. The largest class of actions performed by the dreamer is that of movement, which includes all changes in location whether by riding, walking, running, jumping, climbing or falling. One out of every three recognized activities is of this type. Apparently sleep permits greater freedom of movement to the dreamer. Contrary to popular expectations, however, falling, floating and flying under one's own power do not often occur. Customarily the dreamer moves from place to place by conventional means. His excursions are usually limited to his home environment; rarely does he travel in foreign lands or strange places.

Passive activities such as talking, sitting, standing, watching, looking and seeing are very common in dreams, accounting for one-quarter of all activities. In fact, what strikes one most about dreams is the absence of strenuous activities. The dreamer does things which do not require a great deal of effort. Such commonplace waking pursuits as working, buying and selling are virtually non-existent in dreams. Even drinking and eating occur very infrequently.

Manual and bodily activities, although not frequently represented in dreams, show considerable diversification, yet even here many of the common chores of waking life are omitted. Typing, sewing, ironing, working with tools, repairing something and a host of other daily pursuits are not found in the hundreds of dreams studied. Cooking, cleaning house, making beds and washing dishes are the only domestic activities found,

and each of these occurs but once. Bathing, washing and groom-
ing are also very infrequent. In contrast, swimming, dancing
and playing games occur with greater frequency. The lesson to
be learned from this analysis is that in our dreams we rarely
engage in the routine duties of life. When we are being ener-
getic, it is in the service of pleasure. The world of dreams does
not duplicate the workaday world.

Women are more passive in their dreams than are men. If
we divide dream activities into the two classes of *passive* which
includes looking, sitting, talking, standing and the like, and
active which includes running, driving a car, swimming, dancing, playing ball and similar actions, then women have far
fewer of the active ones in their dreams as compared with men.
Taking only the most strenuous activities performed by men
and women in their dreams, the men's list includes unloading
heavy steel rails, digging for ore, working on a boiler, scaling
the side of a building, fist fighting and rowing a boat, while
the women's list includes moving beds, mixing batter, sweeping
stairs, sorting out flowers, taking clothes from a line and carrying dishes. It is obvious from these two lists that the activities
of men require a greater expenditure of energy than those performed by women. Although dreams reveal that women are
more passive than men they do not tell us the reason for this
difference. It may be because women are physically weaker than
men or it may be because women think of themselves as being
more passive and phlegmatic. Men whether by nature or by
self-conception appear to have an active orientation while
women appear to have a passive one.

Rather large differences between individual dreamers in respect to the amount of strenuous activity displayed are found. An example of a passive dreamer is William.

William is a talented young musician who has been playing in orchestras since an early age, and consequently, did not have an opportunity to engage in games and sports with other boys while he was growing up. He is shy and sensitive, although not abnormally withdrawn, and his natural warmth and affection attract people to him. He controls his emotions, tends to reject sexuality, and feels uneasy with girls. He likes people, and rarely shows any aggression. He is attached to his mother and slightly antagonistic toward his father.

William sits, looks, listens, converses, walks or runs, and rides in eleven of his seventeen dreams. Other dream characters do a lot of different things but William usually just watches. In one dream, for example, he is attending a meeting in a gymnasium but he is sitting apart from the group and does not feel that he belongs. One of the boys starts to go up in an elevator at the side of the gym and is attacked by a husky man.

The attacker hustles his victim into the elevator and the elevator begins to go up and down rapidly. The boys of the group rush to the elevator in an attempt to stop it. Many of them become twisted in the cables as they try to pull it down. Girls now join in the struggle. Most of them fall into a swimming pool where they are pulled to safety by the remaining members of the group. I do not help in the rescue and receive disparaging glances from the others. I pull a blind girl from the pool and then walk away.

The dreamer acts only after he has been criticized by the group and then pulls just one girl to safety before withdrawing.

In six dreams, William is riding in an automobile but in only one of these does he do the driving. Usually he is a passenger and sits in the back seat.

The passivity that William shows in his dreams is in keeping with his passivity during waking life. One has the impression that he does not have a great amount of available energy because his sexual and aggressive impulses are so rigidly inhibited. Some of the inhibited sexuality does express itself in tenderness but except for this, there are few outlets for his impulses. Even in his dreams William can only infrequently act out his blocked impulses.

The cause of this rigid control is fear. William is afraid of what might happen to him should he permit his vital urges free expression. This is revealed especially well in one dream in which he is making love to two girls.

Suddenly a young, well-built and very handsome man appears and rushes madly and threateningly up the aisle toward me.

The dreamer escapes in a milk truck and meets an orchestra conductor and his wife who are concerned about his safety. The orchestra conductor expresses sympathy but warns the dreamer not to involve himself in any more such episodes in the future. This dream shows that William's erotic desires are kept in leash by fear of punishment from young men of his own age and from older men of his father's age.

By contrast with the pallid, passive dream behavior of William, Gene is a vigorous young male animal. In thirteen of his fourteen dreams he engages in some form of strenuous activity. He wrestles, shoots, climbs a cliff, skis, paints, catches a turtle and stamps on it, pulls a dog from a pond, rides a horse, tackles another man, forces his way out of a wrecked truck and at the same time helps to extricate a friend, and has intercourse with a girl. Gene's vitality pours forth in an inexhaustible stream. When, for instance, he encounters an old friend he rushes up and tackles him with all the unrestrained joy of an affectionate dog. When he is angry he seizes a gun and shoots the offending person. And when he is sensually aroused, he does not merely embrace a girl, as William does, but proceeds to have intercourse with her.

In waking life Gene is as different from William as they are in their dreams. Gene belongs to that large group of robust young American men who go all out for sports, competition, tinkering with engines, hunting and fishing, and a relatively free sex life, and who shun anything that is intellectual or aesthetic. William is an intellectual aesthete, physically soft, timorous and tender. Gene is practical-minded. He likes to work with his hands, develop his physique, and compete with his peers. Although both young men were college students at the time they were studied, Gene was a near-failure while William was a good student. Gene did not like his schoolwork and was eager to withdraw from college, get a position in a factory and work his way up to be a factory superintendent.

These two cases illustrate how dream actions reflect the contrasting personalities of two young men. They also point out another feature of dreams that is important for understanding the dreamer, namely, the dreamer's role as watcher or as doer. A person may be a mere observer in his dreams, as William is, or he may be an active participant, as Gene is. A watcher obtains vicarious pleasure from seeing others do what he would like to do without running any of the risks of actual participation. This is the reason why we enjoy movies, detective stories, radio serials and novels which deal with crime, war and sex. Many a writer from the golden age of Greek drama down to the latest Mickey Spillane mystery story has made his fame and fortune by writing about sex and aggression.

The difference between the watcher and the doer is illustrated by the following dreams collected from two young men. In the first dream the dreamer is a spectator, in the second one he is an active participant.

I went to a swimming pool with my mother and some young child. We sat on the bench and watched girls swim. I got up and left mother and sat on another bench by myself. I recognized some of the girls, and paid special attention to one that was very attractive. Everyone started to leave the pool. Mother and the young child left with the girl swimmers. But the girl I liked didn't pass by.

I was in swimming with a girl friend. We played around in the water, ducking each other and swimming together. I could feel her pert little body against mine as we kissed each other.

The first dreamer is tied to his mother's apron strings although there is an indication that he is beginning to assert his independence when he leaves his mother and sits on another bench. Even so he only succeeds in *looking* at the girl who attracts him and they never do get together. His impulses are held in check by his conscience. The second dreamer suffers from no such restraint. He and his girl have a wonderful sensual time in the water.

In conclusion, it may be stated that the analysis of dream actions tells us something about the energetics of behavior, the kind of activities in which the energy is utilized, the nature of the obstacles which impede the flow of energy, and the amount of energy available to the individual.

DREAM EMOTIONS

Some dreams are such delightful fantasies that it is disappointing to wake up and find it was only a dream, while others are such terrifying nightmares that it is a relief to discover that they really did not happen. Between the two extremes of fantasy and nightmare there are many degrees of pleasure and displeasure. Some dreams contain both feelings; others appear to be without any emotional color at all.

Unpleasant dreams are more numerous than pleasant ones, and as one get older the proportion of unpleasant dreams increases.

If dreams are classified according to the particular emotion experienced by the dreamer, fear is more common than anger and sadness is more common than happiness. The unpleasant emotions of fear, anger and sadness are twice as frequent as the pleasant emotions of joy and happiness. Dreaming on the whole is not a pleasurable pastime.

When individual dreams series are analyzed, wide differences in the proportion of pleasant dreams are found. In some series only one or two dreams are pleasant, and in others, pleasant dreams predominate. James, for instance, reported that ten of his sixteen dreams were enjoyable. The subject matter of these ten dreams are making love to a girl in two dreams, playing softball, being admitted to medical school, wishing good luck to a candidate for public office, buying magazines in a drug-store, being home from the Army, being back in the Army with his friends, organizing a sabotage campaign against the Germans and leading a revolt against the Army.

James gets pleasure from a variety of activities—social, athletic, sexual and aggressive. His energy discharges itself easily and smoothly, nor does one find in his dreams that quality of impulsiveness which seems to be the mark of an inhibited person. His impulses flow within channels defined by fairly conventional standards. James does not feel anxious when he revolts against authority, as he does in one dream, or when he makes love to a girl, as he does in several, because he does not have a rigid, demanding conscience. James is one of those rare individuals who is able to express his impulses without feeling guilty. In waking life he is a sanguine, exuberant young man. He likes to play baseball, had a good time in the Army, finds people interesting, enjoys girls and thinks his parents are wonderful. He says that his mind is untroubled and that the future looks bright. He is the sort of person who likes to drink a glass of milk and eat a piece of cake before going to bed. His chief worries are making satisfactory grades in college, gaining admission to medical school, and supporting a wife. He admits that he is lazy. James' dreams convey an impression of a happy go-lucky, uninhibited youth, which in truth, he is.

Happy dreams do not necessarily reflect a happy disposition. Our next dreamer, Jane, has a number of dreams that are very pleasing because in all of them she is achieving success. She is loudly applauded for making a brilliant speech, acclaimed for her skill as a dressmaker, envied by other girls for her popularity with boys, gratified by her success as a schoolteacher and pleased by her expert performance as an ice skater. Her need for attention is so great that in two dreams she has her family killed off for the sole purpose of attracting sympathy to herself. Actually, Jane is a retiring girl who has marked feelings of inferiority and a sense of her own worthlessness. Jane's unpleasant dreams, although they are in the minority, more nearly represent the true state of affairs. In one dream she is apprehensive because she thinks she is going to be asked to sing and she knows she cannot sing, and in another she is elected beauty queen but is unable to get to the center of the stage before another person is chosen. Jane is really an unhappy person who tries to compensate during sleep for her waking unhappiness by imagining that she is a successful, outstanding and admired person. Her pleasant dreams are more like daydreams with their conquering-hero theme than they are like nocturnal ones.

When we compare Jane's dreams with those of James, an important psychological difference is noted. Jane's happy dreams conform to a single type—they are all success stories—whereas James' pleasurable dreams display a great deal of variation. Jane concentrates all of her energy on achieving a single goal, while James deploys his energy in various directions. Furthermore, and this is the crucial difference, Jane compensates in her dreams for what she wants but does not have during waking life while James lives out his impulses in a regulated way just as he does when he is awake. Jane is an *autistic* person, that is, she gratifies her wishes in a fanciful unrealistic fashion. By comparison, James is *realistic*. He is on friendly terms with his needs, recognizes them for what they are, and proceeds to gratify them in a lifelike manner. His dreams are not improbable and magical as Jane's are, but rather convey an impression of verisimilitude.

Let us turn now to consider an unpleasant series. Peter has only one completely pleasant dream out of the twenty in his collection. Ten of his dreams are distinctly unpleasant and nine are both pleasant and unpleasant. Anger, fear and anxiety are his predominant dream emotions. Aside from the fact that anger is aroused principally by other males, either younger or the same age, his anger is not focused on any particular individual but is directed against various people. The causes for the dreamer's anger are also quite varied, consisting of injury to his person, public embarrassment, interference, mistreatment of his car, rejection by girls and other types of frustration.

In five of the dreams Peter restrains his anger, and in six he expresses it overtly, sometimes quite brutally, as in this violent dream.

He [the dreamer's friend] grabbed the guy and took hold of his skin at his abdomen in both hands and ripped it apart and just kept pulling the skin which peeled off like a rabbit being skinned. He pulled all the skin off, even the skin of the face and head, in two pieces and threw it down. I was shocked and revolted. The blood started to ooze out of the fat and made droplets which increased in size. He was still alive and the most horrible sight, it seemed, that I had ever seen.

Peter's sadistic cruelty also shows itself in a dream in which he fights with a fellow worker.

I grabbed his arm without thinking and he took a swing at me. I warded it off with my left arm and lost my temper completely.

I literally threw him into the sink then. The sinks are about three feet square and he landed in the right compartment. He went in head first, his head striking the wire rack in the bottom, and his shoulders and trunk being doubled up, with his feet and legs sticking up onto the drainboard. He lay that way, sort of twitching and stunned. He had lit on the left frontal area of his head and his glasses were knocked loose and were lying under his head, but they were not broken. He had an ugly bruise and a few cuts from the wire rack on his forehead but no blood came from them.

Even when there is no overt discharge of anger in aggressive action the dreamer has to work hard to control his temper. When a young boy puts sand in his coffee Peter says, "I got very angry. I could feel my temper rising within me, and expected to blow my top anytime. There was some restraining influence within me, though." When his two buddies wreck his car, he comments, "I had the feeling of a strong inner conflict as I stood there and didn't trust myself to say much." When his anger does break through into action it is an emotional eruption of pent-up aggression which is out of all proportion to the instigating stimulus.

Anxiety and fear are also prominent in Peter's dreams, and these emotions are also caused by a diversity of circumstances. In six dreams the anxiety or apprehension is produced by threat of bodily harm or by physical disorders. The dangerous situations consist of a boat tipping over, being shot at by Russian soldiers, a pile of logs about to roll over on him, and hitting the ground while flying. In one dream he is terrified because he catches some strange malady that causes his hair to fall out, and in another he is extremely anxious because his teeth drop out. Anxiety is also caused by damage to his watch and to his car, by watching a boy being skinned alive and by strangling a dog. He is also made apprehensive by a premonition that his girl is seriously ill, and by the anger of a woman friend who is about to hit him after he has patted her playfully on the buttocks.

When we look for common elements in these dreams, three major causes for anxiety stand out: (1) physical danger and damage to his own person and destruction of his personal possessions, (2) display of aggression, and (3) loss of love or love object.

Peter's anxiety and anger are intimately related. His brutal and destructive impulses which constantly threaten to get out of control, and sometimes do, actually terrify Peter because they threaten his safety and deprive him of love. He is a victim of a conscience that is so demanding that it will not permit him to drain off his anger in normal ways. Hate piles up behind the dam of a stern conscience until the pressure becomes too great, the dam bursts, and there is an outpouring of vitriolic sadism. Naturally he feels guilty when this happens, and his conscience becomes even more vigilant against a recurrence of brutal action. Consequently Peter goes round and round on a never-ending circle of hate and terror.

From these examples it can be seen that the emotions experienced during dreams yield important information about the personality and conceptions of the dreamer.

COLOR IN DREAMS

One of the most puzzling questions about dreams is why some dreams are in color while others lack color. This question has been studied from many angles, but no satisfactory answer has yet been found. We know that about one dream in three is colored or has some color in it. We also know that a few people dream entirely in color, that more people never experience color in dreams, and that the remainder which constitutes a majority of dreamers sometimes see color in their dreams.

We have tried to determine the significance of color in dreams by comparing chromatic dreams with achromatic dreams, but there seems to be no difference in meaning between them. We have also compared people who dream entirely in color with those who never dream in color, hoping to find some personality characteristics that would differentiate the groups, but no differences have appeared. We have even tried to determine whether a particular color, red, for example, has any fixed symbolic significance when it occurs in dreams. Does it signify passion, as some people think? Our search has been fruitless. The same color may have quite different meanings in different dreams. Green, for instance, can symbolize vigor, or it can symbolize illness.

We have come to the conclusion that color in dreams yields no information about the personality of the dreamer. It is merely an embellishment on the dream and does not signify anything in itself.

In this chapter we have made a quick survey of what normal people dream about. We have seen that each of the four major components of a dream helps us to understand the personal significance of dreams. Settings, characters, actions and emotions are visible projections of what is on the dreamer's mind. They are vehicles of thought bearing messages from the innermost realm of the mind.

3   Dreams of Sex and Aggression

ACCORDING TO Freud dreams represent the fulfillment or attempted fulfillment of wishes. He believed that the two principal wishes or impulses gratified in dreams are those of sex and aggression. During sleep the normal controls of waking life over the expression of these impulses are suspended and the dreamer is able to represent in fantasy what he would not ordinarily do in actuality. We have no quarrel with Freud's theory since a familiarity with thousands of reported dreams amply confirms the fact that sex and aggression furnish the plots for many of them. We do feel, however, that it is not necessary to consult dreams in order to find out that man is sexually and aggressively inclined, since this is made abundantly clear by all sorts of evidence. What we would like to show in this chapter is that dreams reveal what the dreamer thinks about these basic driving forces, how he proposes to handle them, toward whom they are directed and what consequences the dreamer expects to suffer from expressing them.

SEX DREAMS

We direct our attention first to sex dreams and the examples we shall present are mostly dreams in which a nocturnal emission occurs. This type of dream interests us because the occurrence of an orgasm shows unmistakably that the dream is a sexually motivated one.

Although nocturnal emissions do not account for a very large proportion of the total number of orgasms experienced by males, about 85 per cent of the male population will experience one or more "wet dreams" during his life according to the Kinsey study. The highest incidence of sex dreams occurs during the late teens and diminishes with age. Nocturnal emission dreams are most common with college students. Surprisingly enough a few people derive all of their sexual gratification in dreams. "By nearly all moral philosophies nocturnal emissions provide the one form of sexual outlet for which the individual is least responsible and therefore is the least condemned" (Kinsey).

The most direct way of representing sexual thoughts in dreams is to have images of making love and engaging in sexual relations. There are dreams of this kind which are completely unembellished and consist of a single image. "I dreamed I was having sexual intercourse with a girl and woke up having an emission," or "I dreamed my girl and I were engaged in passionate petting and I had an ejaculation." Such dreams show pretty clearly that the dreamer has only one idea in mind, that of sexual gratification. He is imbued with a compelling desire to release a physiological tension in an efficient, straightforward manner. Nor is he particularly concerned with whom he is having sexual relations or with the tender emotion of love. One young man dreamed that he was having relations with a detached female organ as though to say "this is the only part of a woman which interests me."

Sex dreams are rarely so simple and unadorned. Usually the sex impulse is framed in a larger, more complicated picture, the analysis of which yields considerable knowledge about the dreamer's total conception of sexuality and all of its ramifications in his personality. Biologically the sex impulse is of the greatest importance and psychologically its energy saturates many of our thoughts. Let us consider some of the sexual imagery in dreams and what it means for understanding human nature.

Many sex dreams occur in a recreational setting where sensual pleasure is in order and where bothersome inhibitions are temporarily discarded. An amusement park, with its fun house, roller coaster, merry-go-round and flying horses, makes an almost ideal setting for conveying the conception that sex really is a lot of fun. This conception is brought out in the following dream of a young man.

I was at an amusement park with several male friends. The booths were attended by gorgeous-looking girls and we decided to separate to see what we could do for ourselves. I went up to one of these beautiful girls, and asked her where she lived, walked away, then returned and asked her if I could take her home that night. She said I could and just after that I remember going on the merry-go-round. When the park closed, I called for her. We got into a car and drove to her apartment. She asked me in and told me to wait until she changed into something more comfortable.

Observe in this dream that the dreamer is hesitant about making advances to a girl. After asking her where she lives he walks away, but returns later to make a date. He leaves again but his rising sexual tension as depicted by the ride on a merry-go-round brings him back to the girl. The fact that the dream ends before any sexual consummation has occurred also shows the dreamer's reluctance to achieve the desired goal.

The same amusement park setting is used by a man old enough to be the former dreamer's father.

I dreamed that I was on a picnic in an amusement park with some other men my age. I suggested that we all ride the roller coaster for a thrill but they decided not to, saying they were too old. I then decided to ride the coaster by myself but the ticket seller was reluctant to sell me a ticket. I persuaded her at length and boarded the roller coaster. I finished the ride and remained aboard for another ride. I was thrilled when I speedily descended the hills and was forced to gasp for breath. After the second ride I awoke.

In this dream, the woman ticket seller does not want to permit the dreamer to enjoy the thrills of youthful excitement, although in the end she relents. The exertion of sensual indulgence causes him to gasp for breath, as it might an older man.

A bar makes another appropriate background for sensual indulgence since that is what it is used for in waking life. Drinking, as is well known, dissolves one's moral inhibitions and stimulates the sexual appetite. This is brought out in the next dream.

I had walked in a bar with very dark lighting and was conscious of music and a few people about me. I sat at the bar and ordered a drink and immediately I noticed a plain-faced blonde at the bar a few stools away from me. I moved over and began to talk to her and it wasn't long before I began fondling her. Shortly I was having intercourse with her and woke up after the ejaculation.

Party dreams almost always reflect a sensualized conception although they are not always as orgiastic as the following one.

I dreamed my fraternity had a gala party for the entire campus. As the party got under way, all the fellows and girls paired off and began engaging in sexual intercourse.

Sensuality may also be represented in the imagery of climate, as exemplified by this striking nocturnal emission dream.

In the dream, I found myself lying in bed in the early hours of the morning. It was a cold, dull morning and I seemed to feel a chill run through my body. Suddenly the sun rose and the room seemed to fill with warmth. It was during this period that I had an ejaculation.

A change in the climate is used by the following dreamer to symbolize a change in her feelings.

I dreamed that a boy friend came to see me and brought me a diamond engagement ring. We went for a long ride. It started at the dorm and there was a lot of snow around, but somewhere along the line the scene changed to a tropical climate.

This dream closely resembles one reported by a young man in which an orgasm occurs when the scene changes from winter to summer.

Closely related to climate and weather as emblems of erotic feeling is the geographical setting in which the dream is laid. A jungle, Florida, "out West," Africa and other locations which are warm or wild places or regions of the country which are regarded as vacation lands may serve to frame the dreamer's conception of sexuality. Here is a pretty dream of this type.

My dream started with my arrival in India or some other hot country. After arriving I took a trip on camels across the desert. I came to an oasis which turned into a beautiful well-planned garden. It had many flowers, beautiful vine-covered arches and many colored flower gardens. I found myself at a pedestal in this garden getting married to a girl friend.

This dream is less primitive and more romanticized than the other dreams that have been presented. The imagery of the oasis which turns out to be a well-planned garden and getting married before a pedestal shows the orderly and controlled approach that this young man takes toward the gratification of his erotic needs.

A writer will often heighten the effect of a story by having the mood of his characters reflect itself in the landscape. The violent storm in *King Lear* is an example of this literary device. The dreamer makes use of the same artifice. His inner turbulence may manifest itself in the churning of the sea, volcanic eruptions, thunder and lightning, tidal waves, earthquakes and other inclemencies of nature. In one dream a young man sees himself on a cliff at the base of which the sea is churning and dashing among the rocks. This dream culminates in sexual intercourse.

As we pointed out in the preceding chapter the automobile is a common object in dreams. It represents the dreamer's conception of power and potency and often symbolizes sexual energy as the following nocturnal emission dream shows.

I was driving a new Buick convertible. I attempted to lower the top but was unsuccessful for the latches holding the frame down would not release. I drove on down the highway only to find myself in a very confusing traffic jam. At this point in the dream I had an emission.

Other conceptions of the sex impulse that make use of cars are a car on fire, crashing a red light, not being able to put on the brakes, skidding off the road, and having a wreck. One young man dreamed that the hood raised of its own accord and the engine appeared as if it wanted to fly out. He goes on to report:

Quickly I jumped upon the hood and tried to hold it down. At first I was very successful but as my strength ebbed, the force of the hood against me became stronger. I was fighting a losing battle and just as the engine was about to break loose, I woke up.

It is pretty apparent that this lad is fighting a losing battle against an eruption of sexual tension.

The airplane is another symbol of sexuality, since in addition to its power and speed it is able to simulate the rise and fall of the sexual urge by ascending and descending. Machinery too, may be used to represent the sex impulse. In one sex dream a young man was using a power lawn mower prior to having an emission.

We noted earlier that stairways are a popular dream locale. We find now that going up and down stairs or climbing a ladder is associated with erotic pleasure. In our collection of dreams there are a large number of stairway or ladder dreams which are openly sexual in character. This is just one of many.

I dreamed that I was chasing a girl up and down some steel spiral steps. I finally caught her and had intercourse. A nocturnal emission occurred.

In other dreams of this type the dreamer is making love to a girl while climbing stairs, the dreamer is the object of sexual advances after he has mounted the stairs, and the dreamer feels a ladder expand and contract as she climbs to the top. A young girl dreamed repeatedly of walking down the cellar stairs and touching the furnace which immediately blows up. It is not hard to see that this is a symbol of erotic fulfillment. An unusual stairway dream is one reported by a young man.

I dreamed that I was walking up a steep, narrow flight of stairs and kept walking for several hours. I had great difficulty climbing the stairs, and as I neared the top, the stairs seemed to start winding. Finally I reached the top and entered a room. It appeared to be a bedroom. I saw a man and woman on the bed engaged in intercourse. I left the room and walked down the long flight of stairs with a strange feeling.

Here the dreamer watches rather than participates in the sexual activity, which suggests that he may be reviving a childhood memory or fantasy of seeing or hearing his parents indulging in coitus. Such experiences are not at all rare, especially when a baby or young child shares a bedroom with his parents.

Why should going up and down stairs or ladders symbolize

sexuality? For the same reason that airplanes do. They involve ascension and descension, which is one of the principal features of the sex impulse.

Under the influence of religious morality civilized man is prone to look upon sex as animalistic and believe that in order to lead a good life it is necessary for him to control or suppress his animal nature. In view of this conception it is not surprising to find that animals appear in dreams as the embodiment of unleashed sexual vitality. Representation by animals is called theriomorphy and dreams which contain animals are called theriomorphic dreams. Two classes of animals may be distinguished, domesticated animals such as the dog, horse and cat, and wild animals. Domesticated animals appear more frequently in dreams than wild animals do. The three most popular dream animals are horses, dogs and cats in that order.

The horse has long been a leading figure in theriomorphy and his numerous qualities have been celebrated in legend, poetry and fiction. One of the loveliest allegories in which the horse figures is found in Plato's *Phaedrus*. Socrates is speaking

"As I said at the beginning of this tale, I divided each soul into three—two horses and a charioteer; and one of the horses was good and the other bad; the division may remain, but I have not yet explained in what the goodness or badness of either consists, and to that I will now proceed. The right-hand horse is upright and cleanly made; he has a lofty neck and an aquiline nose; his color is white and his eyes dark; he is a lover of honour and modesty and temperance, and the associate of right opinion; he needs no touch of the whip, but is guided by word and admonition only. The other is a crooked lumbering animal, put together anyhow; he has a short thick neck; he is flat-faced and of a dark colour, with grey and blood-shot eyes; the mate of insolence and pride, shag-eared and deaf, hardly yielding to whip and spur. Now when the charioteer beholds the vision of love, and has his whole soul warmed through sense, and is full of the prickings and tick-lings of desire, the obedient steed, then as always under the government of shame, refrains from leaping on the beloved; but the other, heedless of the pricks and of the blows of the whip, plunges and runs away, giving all manner of trouble to his com-panion and the charioteer, whom he forces to approach the beloved and to remember the joys of love."

One could hardly hope to find a more beautiful description of the three main components of man's personality—his primitive, vital impulses, his conscience or idealized self, and his reason.

The horse in dreams rarely symbolizes the idealized self; rather like the mythical centaur the dream horse is a pristine symbol of wild, lawless, licentious animal passion. More spe-cifically the horse usually signifies masculine sexuality since he is a large, powerful creature of great vitality and alarming im-pulsiveness. Interestingly enough the horse appears about twice as often in the dreams of women as in those of men.

Unquestionably one of the pleasures of horseback riding in waking life is the erotic stimulation which the rider receives. A man who was riding a horse in his dreams observed that the ris-ing and falling in the saddle resembled the movements in sexual intercourse. Brill reports that a patient of his neighed at the time of ejaculation. In one unusual dream a young woman dreamed that she was riding in a race on the underside of a horse which suggests the customary coital position of the woman.

In women's dreams the horse is often depicted as an attacker which conveys the conception of rape. The following dream appears to be of this order.

I was in a dark forest picking flowers but I was soon bored so I lay down on the soft green grass. A black and white striped horse broke through the window and carried me away rather roughly.

The breaking of a window symbolizes the dreamer's conception of defloration while the black and white horse embodies the dreamer's conception of sex as having a good and bad side. The black and white horse recalls a dream reported by a middle-aged woman in which there were two horses, one black, the other white. A black horse chased her up to her bedroom where they got into separate beds. When the dreamer looked across to the other bed the horse had changed into a white horse. This dream suggests that Socrates' allegory still has relevance for the modern mind.

It has already been observed that swimming is a sensual sport, so it is not surprising to find swimming and sex associated in dreams as they doubtless are also in waking life. Sometimes swimming dreams are openly sexual in nature while in other dreams the sensual component is couched in symbolism. A young woman dreamed that she had lost her opal ring while swimming in the lake which made her feel heartbroken. Rings are often used in dreams to convey the idea of the female genitals so that this dream signifies the loss of virginity. A masculine version of the same idea except that a pocketbook is substituted for a ring appears in the following dream.

I was on a beach with my girl and other friends. We had been swimming and were sitting on the beach. My girl was afraid that she would lose her pocketbook and kept saying that she felt certain she would lose it on the beach.

This is a rather humorous dream since the girl's fear is the young man's wish. He wants to have relations with her but instead of dreaming this in an outright manner, he turns it around and says "she is afraid of losing her virginity."

Another ironical dream about swimming is this one reported by a young woman.

The housemother met me at the door late at night. She accused me of going swimming in another end of town. I had been drinking, but I knew I had done nothing wrong even though she thought so.

Since there is nothing bad about swimming in itself the housemother's accusation is hardly appropriate unless swimming stands for a sexual transgression which it does in this dream.

Negroes, Indians and other people who are considered to behave more primitively and to be more sexually promiscuous than Caucasians may appear in the dreams of white people as emblems of assertive sexuality. White women have dreams of being attacked by Negroes. These are rape dreams which are motivated by a desire to be taken sexually by an ardent lover. A less common type of dream is one in which the dreamer is being made love to by a Negro. A young woman who reported a dream of this variety said to herself in her dream, "It certainly is true that colored men are more passionate than white men and I like the way they kiss better than white men do."

White men, on the other hand, often envy Negroes for their impressive sexual organs and virility, a feeling that contributes markedly to the white man's unreasonable prejudice against Negroes. The conception of the Negro as an oversexed person helps to explain why colored men are often accused of sexual attacks on white women. This state of affairs is made quite explicit in a dream in which the dreamer and his wife have gone to the park for a picnic.

I left my wife sitting on a park bench reading a magazine and had started down the street a few feet when I happened to glance across the street and saw a Negro walking across in such a direction as to pass near my wife. At first glance he seemed to be wearing shorts but when he came directly opposite me I could see that what appeared to be shorts was nothing but a loin cloth partially covering his genital organs. I stopped and watched him, growing more angry by the second. I had the feeling that if my wife looked up from her book and saw him that I would certainly give him a beating. She didn't look up, however, although the Negro passed within a few feet of her. The Negro was a well-built specimen with large genitals.

In reporting this dream the dreamer volunteered the information that he and his wife had been trying without success to have a child and this had made him feel that he was not much of a man. He is afraid that his wife will leave him for a more virile male.

As we said at the beginning of this chapter the dreamer's conception of his sex impulse may be that of a physiological tension in need of periodic discharge like the turning on of a faucet or his conception may be more psychologically related to his total personality. This difference in conceptions is illustrated by two dreams, the first of which equates sexual gratification with the opening of a door.

My sister's girl friend came in the front door and smiled at me. She continued on through the living room and I arose from my chair and followed her. She walked through a hallway and into the bathroom of our home and closed the door. I opened it. At this point a seminal discharge occurred and I awoke.

How barren and mechanical this dreamer's conception appears when placed alongside the next dream, one of the most colorful sex dreams in our collection.

I and four or five companions of the same age got out of our car at some park. It was winter and the place was abandoned. Ice was all over the ground. We walked across an open area and as we passed through some passageway we found ourselves threading our way down a sunny mountain trail looking for gold. We noticed other groups coming after us. We finally came out into a great field with a jungle in the distance. We noticed small animals resembling pigs running around. As we got into the jungle proper, which was very light and sunny, we saw all sorts of wild life, lions, giraffes, pythons standing out in my mind. For safety we decided to climb trees. I first climbed a small tree but found it was not safe enough so I came down and began to climb a large tent pole which I had not noticed before. As I did so, I had a nocturnal emission.

This dreamer has an artistic conception of erotic fulfillment which is represented by an elaborate vein of scenic imagery.

In concluding this section on sex dreams we should like to emphasize again the fact that the sex impulse, or for that matter any impulse, may express itself in many ways and that the particular form which a dreamer adopts is determined by his conception of the impulse. If he conceives of sex as something dirty he will employ dream imagery consonant with this idea.

If he views it as a dangerous alien force it will appear so in his dreams. The detection of basic impulses is not important since all people have them. What we need to discover if we are to understand a person and his conduct is what he thinks about his impulses. For it is his idea of an impulse that determines his behavior and not the impulse itself.

AGGRESSIVE DREAMS

Sex is one basic impulse that is built into man and aggression is another. This is as it should be if man is to survive and reproduce. Like sex, however, aggression is frowned upon by society except when it is officially sanctioned as in warfare or in self-defense. The suppression and control of these two powerful forces means that they will seek and find devious outlets. One such outlet is dreams so it should not surprise us to find considerable aggression in dreams as we do. In line with the general thesis of this book, however, we are more interested in the dreamer's conceptions of aggression than we are in the mere presence of aggression.

An aggressive encounter has three major components. They are the person who commits the aggression, called the *aggressor,* the person against whom the hostility is directed, called the *victim,* and the nature of the aggressive act. We have analyzed hundreds of aggressive encounters in dreams for these three components and here briefly are our findings.

There are two principal ways of expressing aggression in dreams. These are physical assault and verbal attack. Outright murder is infrequent, as are stealing, destroying someone's property and disobedience. Male dreamers prefer physical aggression while female dreamers prefer verbal aggression. In overall amount of aggression, men exceed women, which is in accord with the prevalent notion that men whether by nature or by cultural influences are more aggressive than women.

Who are the victims of these aggressive encounters? More often than not the dreamer himself is the victim. Where this is the case the dreamer tells us, in effect, that it is not he who feels aggressive but rather it is the world outside which is peopled with enemies. These enemies have it in for him because he has done something wrong, because he has dared to assert himself, or because people are just plain mean.

The enemies in male dreams are predominantly other men while in female dreams they are about equally divided as to sex. However if we consider only enemies that are a generation older than the dreamer, then it is found that women dreamers receive aggression from older females more often than from older males while it is just the reverse for men dreamers. Since older characters in dreams usually stand for the parents of the dreamer, it may be said that women conceive of the mother as their chief enemy while men conceive of the father as their chief enemy. The dreamer is more likely to be the victim of aggression from older characters than he is to aggress against them. In his hostile encounters with characters his own age, the dreamer gives and receives about an equal amount of aggression.

When the dreamer initiates an attack on another person, male dreamers choose male opponents and women divide their aggression between both sexes. All things considered men cast other men in the dual role of attackers and victims while women attack and are attacked equally often by males and females. This state of affairs places a heavy psychological burden upon women since they are never as certain as men are as to who the enemy really is. Putting it in another way, women have to contend with both sexes while men only contend with one sex.

There is more aggression involving strangers than there is involving people who are known to the dreamer. Apparently there is something threatening about a stranger which predisposes one to cast him in the role of an enemy. Moreover, one feels less guilty about fighting with a stranger than he does with a friend or family member. As we have mentioned before, strangers in dreams may represent alien aspects of the dreamer or of people he knows. Accordingly a fight with a stranger may really be a fight with oneself or with a friend.

Dreamers differ greatly in the amount of aggression expressed in their dreams. Some people rarely have aggressive dreams while others dream almost exclusively of hostility. There are also wide differences in the number of aggressions initiated by the dreamer and the number directed against him as well as in the severity of the aggressive acts. Some dreamers confine their hostility to angry looks or words, others engage repeatedly in physical assault.

These differences among dreamers may be illustrated by the dreams of two young men of similar background and experiences. In sixteen dreams collected from the first dreamer, whom we shall call Paul, no aggression is evident. His dreams are happy and gay, and most of them are about girls. The following dream is typical.

Jane and I were on a cliff overlooking a big rock, a place where we often went this last fall to study and picnic. It was nighttime and Jane was unhappy. The sky was stormy and evil-looking and she seemed to take on the spirit of the weather. I told her not to be sad, "I can fix everything." She asked how. I said, "Watch," and I tilted back her head and kissed her. At once the sky cleared, brightened and stars shone happily. She laughed and was happy.

Paul is truly a man of peace bringing happiness to others. The world, seen through his eyes, is a friendly, comfortable place in which there is no room for ill feeling and hate.

Richard's view of the world is the antipode of Paul's. In his world men are motivated by hate. One kills lest one be killed. In twenty dreams collected from Richard he is involved in fourteen aggressive encounters, seven as aggressor and seven as victim. The encounters are always serious ones. His victims are a young Army acquaintance whom he has arrested, a strange young man whom the dreamer grabs by the leg and throws on a steep roof from which he falls and breaks his neck, a group of black men in a tree at whom the dreamer shoots, soldiers at whom the dreamer is firing, two women whom the dreamer has arrested, a man whom the dreamer rides down on horseback, and a pig which the dreamer shoots to death. The dreamer is aggressed against by men who arrest him, by a black man who jabs at him with a spear, by soldiers who attack him, by a strange young man who chases him, by a woman who holds him prisoner and tries to poison him, by a small boy who knocks him down, and by someone who is about to knife him in the back. Richard is not selective in his choice of victim or aggressor; men, women, children and animals are all involved. Most of them are strangers.

Richard's conception of the world is one of death, destruction and detention, a conception which is expressed in his dreams even when direct aggression is absent. In dreams not involving hostility Richard and other characters have one misfortune after another. A young fellow suffers a painful cramp, Richard gets stuck in a narrow passageway, he is watching a funeral, a man falls over a cliff and Richard's father is killed in a plane crash.

Richard is really at war with himself. It is a war between a stern conscience and volatile impulses in which reason is practically eliminated. This internal conflict is nicely symbolized by a Civil War dream in which Richard is fighting on the side of the South against the North. A civil war is an internal war within a nation and as such is a projection of Richard's inner conflict. The South stands for the rebellious impulses and the North for the law and order of conscience. By finally surrendering to northern soldiers, Richard tells us that he is giving in to his conscience.

Paul and Richard are contrasting character types. For want of assertiveness and pugnacity Paul seems to be more feminine than masculine and this in fact is how he appears to others in waking life. He is a sensitive, aesthetic young man of refined and cultivated tastes. Richard's character is drenched with hostility; life for him is perpetual combat and danger. In only one dream does Richard feel really happy and relaxed. It is one in which he is floating in the air, "like a feather in a breeze" as he puts it. This is sheer fancy, an escape from hostile forces from within and from without, an escape from life itself. Obviously there is no escape for Richard as long as his own personal civil war persists.

Aggression may manifest itself in indirect ways as well as direct ones in dreams. The principal indirect way is for a misfortune to befall a dream character or the dreamer himself. Death, serious illness, injury and accidents are not uncommon in dreams although rarely do these more serious adversities happen to the dreamer. His misfortunes are more apt to be of a trivial nature such as a minor illness, injury or danger.

Why do we call a dream misfortune an indirect way of expressing aggression? We do so on the assumption that everything that happens in a dream expresses an idea in the mind of the dreamer, and that a particular idea exists because it serves some purpose. Suppose a young man dreams that his father dies, as Richard did. Richard did not have to dream this in the sense that it was forced upon his mind by some external agent. It was his own idea that his father should die in an airplane crash. Richard wanted his father to die but he could not bring himself to perpetrate the murder by his own hands. By having him killed in an accident Richard evades all responsibility for his father's death and thereby salves his conscience.

One young woman dreamed that her whole family, save herself, were swept to their death by a tidal wave. By such a ruse she gets rid of her family and then wallows in self-pity because she is all alone in the world. It reminds one of the story of the young man who killed his father and mother and then pleaded for mercy from the judge because he was an orphan.

Is it not possible that a death dream represents a fear rather than a wish? Is it not perfectly normal for one to be apprehensive about the health and welfare of those close to him and for these apprehensions to find expression in dreams? Yes, it is perfectly normal but this fact does not account for our apprehensions. Everyone will die sometime and the possibility of sudden death is in every street, factory and home so that our minds ought continually to be filled with thoughts of death. But ordinarily one's mind is not obsessed with death. It is only occasionally that we think about it. When we dream about a person's dying and wake up feeling alarmed our alarm springs from the circumstance that we dared to project a wicked thought into a dream. Our anxiety is the result of the dream, not the cause of it.

What about those cases where a person dreams of someone dying who actually is in poor health? We would reply, why doesn't he dream of the person getting well if this is really his wish? After all a person dreams what is on his mind, and if the thought of the ill person getting well is in his orientation he will not dream of death. In fact there are many dreams in which the dreamer does dream of a sick person recovering or even a dead person who comes to life.

Still, not all dreams of death represent murderous impulses. To dream of the death of a person may be the dreamer's way of showing that his feeling for the person has ceased to exist. By the same token to dream of someone returning to life can signify that the dead person has come alive emotionally for the dreamer. This is exemplified in the following dream reported by a young woman who had fallen in love with a man several years after the death of her brother with whom she had a close attachment.

> I dreamed of my dead brother who told me that he had never met Will and that he did not want me to marry Will until he had met him. I told my brother that he had died and could not meet Will. Don [the brother] said he was not really dead.

The young woman reveals in this dream that she is still influenced by her feeling for her brother and that she needs his permission before she can marry. By having Don say in her dream that he is not really dead is equivalent to the dreamer saying, "My brother is still alive in my thoughts." Another young woman whose father had died dreamed that she built a memorial tower in his honor. The tower is a concrete representation of a wish that her father might remain alive in her memories.

Misfortunes visited upon the dreamer represent self-punishment. When a person punishes himself he does so because he feels guilty and the punishment is a way of expiating for a bad thought or a bad deed. Paradoxically, good people punish themselves more than bad people do. This is brought out in the dreams of a young man whom we shall call Robert. Robert is a cheerful, extraverted, friendly and even-tempered person who has been carefully raised in a conventional home. He is a good boy in every sense of the word. His dreams tell another story. In them, fear and despair predominate. He suffers repeated misfortunes and is the victim of aggression from others. These misfortunes occur after he has indulged himself as in the following dream.

I dreamed of a very sumptuous banquet table and myself sitting
before it. The others around the table gazed very fondly and ap-
provingly at me. I was very happy and sensed a lightness and freedom about myself. I took a bite and it stuck in my throat. I felt
the blood rush to my head and stumbled away frightened. I tried
to call for help but when I turned around I discovered I was alone.
I felt like I would soon die.

The sumptuous banquet represents for Robert the pleasures of
the flesh, and when he attempts to satisfy them the stern arm
of conscience exacts its retribution. He is deserted by his
friends and left to die. Desertion is a recurrent theme in his
dreams of which the following one is typical.

I would suddenly find myself standing on the sidewalk in front
of my house. I sensed a pressing loneliness and felt that I was the
only person for miles around. I would look at all the houses and
they would appear dark and foreboding. I suddenly felt like running, but by running I might endanger myself; for moving from
where I was standing had an ominous significance.

Movement means giving in to his impulses. In Robert's eyes
it is better to be lonely than to be wicked. In another dream, he
starts to take a step and becomes deathly ill. "After this," he
says, "I felt content to stand and not move any more." Robert
is immobilized by fear of what might happen should he give
way to his impulses.

The full measure of Robert's despair and hopelessness is
portrayed in the next dream.

I found myself paddling up a river in a small boat. The river
was very narrow and very deep, for I peered over the side and
often felt quite anxious fearing the boat might sink. I paddled
quite aimlessly and easily up the river and as I neared a distant

bend I suddenly felt quite excited and afraid. I seemed to know that up ahead lay something that I must reach and was very dear to me. Yet I knew I could never reach it, for I felt something would stop me. I paddled faster and faster and the faster I paddled the more quickly I slipped back downstream. *I gave up.*

No matter what he tries by his own initiative he fails to achieve. In Robert's dreams, we see the inner picture of a good person. Virtue is not its own reward as so many people believe but rather as Herman Melville with greater perspicacity observes "conscience is the wound."

To sum up this chapter, it may be said that sex and aggression are two potent motivating forces in dreams. In fact an aggressive act or a misfortune occurs in half of the dreams of our extensive collection. Sex dreams are probably as frequent but they are not reported as often because of the shame associated with sex.

As we have said before, however, dreams tell us more about a person than that he is sexually and aggressively driven. They tell us what a person thinks about these basic impulses, what people they are directed against, and how they can best be satisfied. They also yield information about what the dreamer thinks will happen to him should he express his impulses. All in all, sex and aggression dreams illuminate the deeper recesses of the dreamer's mind, since sex and aggression are the two basic motivating forces of thought and behavior.

4 How Dreams Are Interpreted

PROUST, THE great French writer, once observed that it is only by reading a number of books by the same author that we can discover the characteristic and essential traits of that author. So it is with a person's dreams. From a single dream we may learn a few things about the dreamer but not until we have studied a number of his dreams are we able to paint a valid picture of his essential character. It is for this reason that we prefer to analyze a series of dreams of a person rather than to interpret single dreams as is the usual custom among dream interpreters.

In treating a series of dreams, the individual dreams are compared with one another and are put together much as one assembles a jigsaw puzzle. One tries various combinations, fitting this dream with that dream, until all of the dreams are joined together and a meaningful picture of the dreamer emerges. In this method, which we call the dream series method, the interpretation of any one dream is a hunch until it has been verified by falling in place with interpretations made of other dreams. If it does not fall in place the interpretation is considered to be wrong and a new one is sought until one is found that is consistent with the total picture.

Some dreams of a series are easier to interpret than others. Their meaning is right out on the surface of the dream, and they scarcely need to be interpreted at all. We call dreams of this type *spotlight* or *bareface* dreams. Since these dreams provide us with the easiest avenue into the mind of the dreamer we start with them when we begin analyzing a dream series. We go from the simple to the complex by easy steps so that even the most obscure dream ordinarily divulges its message.

Let us illustrate our method by considering a series of dreams recorded by an eighteen-year-old boy. He has recently fallen in love, his first serious attachment, and although he would like to get married immediately he feels that this is out of the question because he is not financially independent. In waking life he constantly thinks of his girl, their happiness together, and their future marriage. It is not surprising that he dreams about her frequently and that his dreams are often of an erotic character.

The first dream of his series reveals his romantic notions as well as a lot of other things about the dreamer.

I was sitting on a throne of gold surrounded by beautiful girls. The girls kept pawing me and I kept chasing them away. Suddenly one girl stood up and came close to me. I was surprised by her good looks. She bent down and kissed me. I felt thrilled. I put my arms around her and picked her up. We danced for a while. I was taken by her hearty manner. She was a most beautiful creature. I went wherever she went. I received a thrill every time she touched me. I wanted her badly. Then we were both floating in the clouds completely nude. We were pleasantly talking and laughing. Suddenly we were dancing and singing. I was extremely happy. I continually kissed her and she reciprocated. We stood arm in arm rolling on.

It is quite apparent that this is a simple wish-fulfillment dream that stops just short of sexual consummation. However, this is not the most important information contained in the dream. How does the dreamer conceive of himself in relation to girls? Although he is an exalted figure seated on a golden throne, he assumes the role of a passive receiver of love and affection from a group of girls. It is they who take the initiative, especially one girl who kisses him. He follows her and is thrilled when she touches him.

This dream poses two questions. What prevents him from consummating his sexual urge? Does he really think of himself consistently as a passive person and of girls as active lovers? The next dream gives us some insight regarding the first question.

I was driving on an open road. I was speeding. My foot was down hard on the accelerator. Suddenly I saw a beautiful girl waiting at the edge of a road for a lift. I tried to stop the car but my foot couldn't find the brake. I frantically looked for the brakes but they had disappeared. Suddenly in front of me on the road was my girl. I wanted to stop the car and suddenly the brakes were in their proper place and I stopped.

The speeding car in this dream as in most dreams represents the power of sexuality while the brakes symbolize control over the sex impulse. When he sees the first girl it looks as though he is not going to be able to control himself, but then his girl appears in his thoughts and he restrains himself. "The brakes were in their *proper* place." The message in this dream is that he does not let himself go with his own girl because his moral sense will not permit him to. When he is tempted to indulge himself with another girl the image of his girl flashes into his mind to restrain his wayward impulses.

It will be observed that the dreamer assumes a more active part in this dream. He is driving a car. Does this mean that the impression of passivity obtained from the first dream is incorrect? Let us see what his other dreams have to say on this question.

In the next dream sensuality is symbolized by swimming in a deep pool.

I dreamed that I went swimming in a deep pool that was not familiar to me. I took all my clothes off and put them on the bank. I began swimming. When I finished I got out of the pool and began looking for my clothes but I couldn't find them. Suddenly I saw a girl holding my clothes and beckoning me to come with her. She began running and I ran after her. She put my clothes in a cave and disappeared.

Disrobing signifies the shedding of one's moral prohibitions. When he tries to find his clothes he discovers that a girl is holding them. She urges him to follow her. Here, as in the first dream, a girl invites him to do something but before he is able to gain his desire she disappears.

The theme of the seductive female is elucidated in rather obvious symbols in the next dream.

My girl friend and I were sitting on a couch in her house. Suddenly she pulled a gun from my pocket and handed it to me. She begged me to shoot her. I was mortified. I ran to the door but she ran after me. I knew that her only wish was for me to shoot her. I pulled the trigger and then I began to laugh.

His girl is begging him to shoot her. Does this mean that he has an idea that his girl really wants to be killed? Not at all. This is a pure sex dream. The gun stands for the dreamer's sex organ and the girl is saying in effect "seduce me." Else why should the dreamer feel mortified and why should he laugh after he pulls the trigger? Mortification and laughter are more appropriate to sensuality than to murder. However, the important feature of this dream is that the girl again takes the initiative.

What do we know about this dreamer at this point? He is a vain, passive, sex-hungry young man who cannot give vent to his urges except when he is made the victim of seduction by a girl. By this stratagem he avoids censure from his conscience.

Another conception of sex and of his girl is portrayed in the following dream.

I was standing in the middle of a large forest. I walked to and fro but I could find no way of returning home. I suddenly felt my foot slip into a muddy quagmire. I began slipping into the mud. I kept sinking in deeper and deeper. Suddenly my girl was at my side. She grabbed at my hands and finally pulled me out and saved me.

Sex is seen as sinking into a muddy quagmire, a conception that sex is dirty. His girl is cast in the part of a rescuer, which is quite a contrast with her role as seducer in the preceding dream. Still it is consonant with his idea that women are strong figures.

There is a new development in this dream—he cannot find his way home. Having become involved in sexuality he is cut off from his family. This anxiety about sex is responsible for most of the psychological growing pains of the adolescent, who thinks that he will become a pariah if he yields to his erotic demands.

Our dreamer's tremendous anxiety expresses itself dramatically in the next dream. This dream is a companion piece to the foregoing one, except that in this one, he appeals unsuccessfully to a male acquaintance.

I was standing near the bank of a river. The surroundings were dark and suspicious and I was afraid. I suddenly felt myself falling into space without ever coming to a halt. Suddenly I plunged into the icy cold water. I could not swim. I cried for help. I heard someone calling and coming toward me. He began laughing at me. I looked at him. He was an old schoolmate of mine whom I detested. He laughed again and said he would let me drown. I screamed and as rapidly as I screamed he laughed. I felt myself drowning. But he wouldn't help me. Then the scene became blank. I plunged into darkness fighting for breath. I was afraid. I felt a pressure against me. I wanted help but received only a bitter laugh. I could see nothing as the water pressed into me.

"Save me" is his pitiful cry, but the detestable male merely laughs derisively as he watches the dreamer drown. The dreamer's conception of males differs from that of females. Men are mean and cruel, women are friendly and helpful.

What happens when both sexes appear in a dream? This question is answered by the following one.

My girl and I were walking through a very familiar park. We were talking and enjoying ourselves when suddenly I found my girl talking to another fellow. I knew not from whence he came. I tried to pull her away but she demanded that I leave her alone. I became worried. I feared that this fellow would steal her. I picked up a rock and hit him over the head, but he wouldn't fall down. I kept on hitting him and he remained standing. Then my girl pushed me away and walked away with my best buddy.

In this dream, the dreamer proves to be a pretty ineffectual fellow. His blows have no effect with the result that he loses his girl to a stronger and more adequate male. Is this what he fears—his impotence as a male, and his inability to compete with other males in a rivalry for love? Let us reserve judgment for the time being.

We come now to a group of dreams that help to fill out the picture of this young man. In these dreams he is the victim of physical or verbal attack by an older man. In five dreams the attacker is his girl's father, in one it is the dreamer's father and in the other four it is an owner of a store, a captain of a ship, a high-school teacher and a dentist respectively. The dreams will be presented in that order. Here is the first one.

I was sitting on a couch in my girl's front room, when my girl's father walked in. He looked at me and sneered. He took a pipe from his pocket and poured the ashes over me. I screamed indignantly but all he did was laugh. Then he stepped on my hat and laughed some more.

There is no doubt about the boy's conception of his prospective father-in-law as depicted in this dream. He feels that the older man has little use for him. Being covered with ashes and having one's hat stepped upon are extremely humiliating since ashes are commonly associated with urine and hats are symbols of the male member. In certain religious rites ashes are scattered over the head of a person as an act of abasement.

What does the dreamer do when he is treated in this contemptible manner? He screams indignantly like a baby instead of defending himself like a man. His girl's father sneers and laughs at him just as the young man did in a previous dream.

Although a self-conception of weakness predominates it is not always found in his dreams. Occasionally he displays a streak of manliness in standing up against an enemy as he does in the next dream.

I was walking in the park with my girl one night. We sat down on the bench and we were kissing when my girl's father strode up and pulled a gun. He threatened me and demanded that my girl go home. We refused and he cursed. I took a stone and hit him. He fell down and we ran away.

In this dream, unlike a preceding one, his blows are effective and the older man falls while the dreamer and his girl flee. We now see why the young man is afraid of the older man. His fear arises from the idea that his girl's father does not want him to make love to his daughter. Whether this is really so or not cannot be learned from dreams nor is it of any material significance in understanding the dreamer. The important point is that the dreamer thinks this is the way the girl's father feels and his thinking it makes him afraid of the older man.

The same theme is developed in the following dream except that our dreamer reverts to his more familiar role of a screaming infant. Notice also that it is the girl who makes the advances as in the former dreams.

I dreamed that I was walking with my girl in the park. She held on tight to my hands and wouldn't let go. She pulled me in the bushes and began kissing me. I was being smothered with kisses when suddenly my girl's father in the form of a fish came up and bit me. I screamed and my girl ran away dazed.

In the next dream, the young man debases himself to the extent of having his girl act as a shield against the murderous father.

My girl and I were riding in a car driven by my girl's father. All of a sudden the car stopped near a bridge. We all got out and walked to the bridge and looked out into the sea. Then my girl's father pulled a gun and told me to jump. The girl implored her father. It did no good. My girl then ran in my path. Her father shot and she fell into my arms.

His idea of women is not only that they shall play the assertive part in making love but also that they shall protect a poor defenseless male like himself against attack from stronger men. This dual conception of women as seductive courtesans and protective mothers is not at all uncommon among men.

His notion that the girl's father hates him for trying to steal his daughter finds embodiment in the next dream.

I found myself running away from something. I was in my girl's backyard and the more I kept running, the more I felt someone was chasing me. But every time I looked around I saw no one. Yet I was certain of being chased. Then I heard someone yell. It was my girl's father telling me not to step on the grass.

He is really running away from his own feelings of guilt for trying to steal another man's loved one. The dreamer is being upbraided by his conscience which is personified by the father.

We begin to suspect that his anxiety concerning the girl's

father may be related to an earlier conception of his own father. This gentleman makes an appearance in the following dream.

I dreamed that one night I was caught stealing an apple from our neighborhood grocer. He took me home and told my father about my acts as a thief. My father took me in his study and forced me to eat all the apples in the house. I could hardly talk, my mouth was stuffed with apples. I began to cry and my father hit me with an apple.

The picture of his own father as a cruel sadistic person is exactly the same as the picture of his girl's father and of the boy who would not save him from drowning. His generalized conception of men is that they are ruthless enemies.

Apples are an emblem of love and stealing them means that he is taking someone's love which does not rightfully belong to him. In former dreams he was stealing a girl's love from her father. Whose love is he taking in this dream? It is reasonable to assume that the apples symbolize his mother's love and that this is why the father is so punitive. What else could he steal that would cause his father to get so angry?

Another version of the same idea is presented in the next dream.

I dreamed I saw a man climbing into a store window. I believed him to be a thief and ran after him. I caught him and after a struggle brought him to a police officer. The thief claimed to be the owner of the store. He proceeded to identify himself and I was told I had made an error. I could not face the man and all he did was laugh. I began to cry and ran away.

A man who is mistaken for a burglar turns out to be the rightful owner of the store. If store stands for mother, as seems highly probable, then this dream says in effect that his mother belongs to his father, who can take possession of her whenever he chooses. Climbing in a store window is a direct representation of sexual intercourse so that the dream has an even more specific meaning, which might be phrased in this way: "It is all right for my father to possess my mother sexually but if I should try it I would be severely punished." He carries this same idea over to his girl and that is why he sees her father as such a menacing figure.

In the following dream the older man is a ship's captain who threatens the dreamer but as in a former dream the punishment is deflected onto his girl. This time, however, the dreamer rushes to her defense and overpowers the attacking captain instead of remaining ineffectual and passive.

I dreamed that I was on a boat sailing on rough waters. The captain was a big mean-looking man. He had a whip in his hand and threatened me. He cursed me and cracked his whip. Then the captain shook his whip at my girl. He hit her with his whip. Blood began spurting. I grabbed the captain and hit him and threw him overboard. My girl ran up to me and kissed me.

This is the only other dream in which the dreamer plays the part of a manly hero.

In the next dream he reverts to his customary role of the fainthearted, inadequate person.

I was playing baseball in a vacant lot. I hit the ball hard and it smashed a window. I tried to run away but my legs would not move. I was glued to the spot. The victim wandered down and to my horror it was an old high-school teacher of mine whom I disliked. He put on his glasses and sneered. He took my baseball bat and struck me. I blacked out.

It is ironical that the teacher deprives the lad of a symbol of his masculine prowess, the baseball bat, and then uses it to punish the dreamer. The smashing of the window suggests the same meaning as climbing in a window, namely a sexual one. In other words the dreamer is punished for expressing his sexuality.

The final dream of this group is a beautiful projection of the dreamer's images of the cruel male and the protective female.

I was sitting in a dentist's chair. The dentist was about to give me gas. I screamed and struggled. I felt the gas taking effect. My body became rigid. A buzzing sounded in my head. Suddenly I was flying in an airplane. A nurse was beside me pleasantly holding my hand. I was not conscious of sound now. The nurse began singing pleasantly. I listened intently. I noticed the dentist piloting the plane. He was unusually tall. He turned around and looked at me. I believe I screamed. The nurse stopped singing. The dentist began coming toward me. I tried to run but it seemed that my feet were glued to the spot. He came closer and closer. Suddenly I awoke.

Can anyone doubt who has read these dreams that they fit together like a jigsaw puzzle and the picture which emerges shows a boy on the verge of manhood who is caught in the web of conflict? That he considers himself to be weak and impotent and unmanly is made abundantly plain. His incestuous longing for his mother gets him into trouble with his father, and this prototypic anxiety disturbs his relationship with a girl which is threatened on every hand by her father. Men are his enemies because he wants something they already possess. Instead of fighting for the object of his desire he usually utters agonizing cries when he is attacked. Lurking behind his infantile behavior, however, is a spark of manliness which might be expected to burst into flame as he grows older and becomes more sure of himself.

His principal conflict consists of a desire to be possessed by a woman versus a dread of retaliation by a man. The manifest characters in the triangle are the dreamer, his girl and her father. This is a replica of an earlier triangle which consisted of the dreamer and his parents. He, like all boys, having gone through a stage of rivalry with the father for the mother's affection and having lost this contest is uncertain of himself when he tries to win the love of a girl his age. This girl has a father who is seen by the dreamer in the same way as he once saw his own father.

In most boys this conflict with the father resolves itself when the boy accepts his father as a model to be emulated rather than as a rival to be vanquished. In our dreamer the conflict has been so poorly resolved that it breaks out again when he falls in love with a girl. New actors, the girl and her father, re-enact the roles once played by the young man's mother and father. For some reason he has not been able to model himself after his father and acquire the confidence and strength necessary to be a dominant and possessive lover.

His inadequacy is felt not only in relation to older men, but also appears in relation to young men as shown by the dream in which his best friend steals his girl. This condition makes his situation even more serious, for assuming that he could change his conception of older men he would still have to contend with his image of stronger young rivals. They would still threaten him with dispossession of a love object and he would feel unable to do anything about it. Men, all men of whatever age, are his enemies. He occupies one of the lowest rungs on the hierarchy of masculinity.

The main defense employed by the dreamer against his enemies is to behave like a child. He cries, screams, faints, is nursed and runs away. In view of this defense it is hardly to be wondered at that he should dream of being dead since this is the ultimate wish of a person who is afflicted with so much anxiety about his ability to face up to the rigorous tests of manhood. The final dream in this series is a death dream.

I was boarding a train for another city. I was about to close the train door when someone beckoned me to get off. I didn't want to get off but some unknown force began to pull me. I was forced to get off and follow this strange person. I followed him up to the sky and there was my grandfather who has been dead for two years. He wept with joy when he saw me.

The death wish, which is symbolized by the dreamer's joining his deceased grandfather in heaven, wins out over the life impulse which is represented by a journey. Although death dreams are not common in young people since the life force is so strong in youth, they do occur in boys and girls who feel completely hopeless and helpless. That our dreamer has such feelings is evidenced by many of his dreams, and is confirmed by this final one.

We have spent a great deal of time with this dream series because we wanted to demonstrate exactly how one goes about extracting maximum meaning from a series of dreams. In this case, as in all cases, the dreams read like chapters in a book.

When put together in order as we have done there is organization, unity and coherence among the dreams. Each dream complements or supplements the other dreams of the series. There is very little left to guesswork since what may seem ambiguous or hidden in one dream is revealed in another dream. Dream interpretations based upon a series of dreams can be very precise and objective if one approaches the task in a scientific manner. And it can yield an amazing amount of basic information about a person if one is willing to follow a few basic rules. Although some of these rules have been alluded to before it may be worth while to review them again.

It is my conviction that anyone who is able to follow a few rules can interpret dreams. Dreams are not mysterious, supernatural or esoteric phenomena. They are not messages from the gods nor are they prophecies of the future. They are not due to something we ate nor are they merely responses to alarm clocks, changes in temperature or bodily movements of the sleeper. They are pictures of what the mind is thinking. Anyone who can look at a picture and say what it means ought to be able to look at his dream pictures and say what they mean. The meaning of a dream will not be found in some theory about dreams; it is right there in the dream itself. One does not read into a dream a meaning that he has learned from some book; rather he reads out of the dream what is there to be read. Any clear-headed person should be able to interpret dreams. The following rules may help him to avoid some of the common mistakes. Let it be noted that the word *clear-headed* has been used. I certainly do not advocate that mentally unbalanced persons should analyze their dreams as a substitute for psychotherapy performed by a qualified therapist. I do believe very firmly, however, that the reasonably well-adjusted person can acquire a great deal of useful information about himself by analyzing his dreams, and it is to this person that the following remarks are directed.

The cardinal rule for understanding dreams is that a dream is a creation of the dreamer's mind. The dreamer is playwright, producer, director, scenery designer, stage manager, prompter, principal actor and audience all at the same time. He writes and prepares the dream for production, sets the stage and designs the costumes, arranges the business and stage effects, provides the props, instructs the actors in the interpretation of their parts, assumes the leading role, does the work of the stagehands, and then sits back to enjoy or suffer through the performance. In short, a dream is a projection of what the dreamer thinks about himself, about other people and about the world.

A dream is not an accurate picture of objective reality and should never be treated as such. It is, however, an accurate picture of reality as it appears to the dreamer. This kind of reality is called subjective reality. Often one's subjective reality does correspond with objective reality, but from dreams alone it is not possible to determine the extent of this correspondence. For example, from the dream series discussed in this chapter, one cannot tell whether the dreamer's father and prospective father-in-law really do treat him cruelly in waking life or whether this is just what he imagines. In any event, we do know that this is how the dreamer pictures his father and his girl's father. It would be the height of folly for a person to say, "He must hate me because he treats me so badly in my dreams."

A second important rule for correct dream interpretation is

that nothing appears in a dream which the dreamer does not put there himself. The dreamer as the creator of a dream is responsible for everything that appears in his dreams. If he dreams it he must have thought it. It has been said that dreaming is egocentric. If by egocentric one means to think only of oneself, the statement is false since dreams are concerned with thoughts about other people and things besides the dreamer. If it is meant that a dream is the product of the dreamer and no one else then the statement is true. However, the same condition holds for waking thought as well. Another person can never think our thoughts for us. We can only think our own thoughts. Some people imagine that other people are putting ideas into their head but this belief is merely the delusion of a disordered mind. Whatever we do or say, whether asleep or awake, is caused by ideas developed out of our own thinking. That is why we say a person is responsible for his dreams and that interpretations should always lead back to the dreamer's mind and personality and not to the outside world. Even when a known external stimulus is acting upon a sleeping person we should ask, "What is the dreamer's conception of this external event?" To proceed by any other course is to invite the disaster of mistaking subjective thought for objective reality.

The third rule is to be aware of the fact that a dreamer may reveal more than one conception of himself or of another person in a single dream or in a series of dreams. Ordinarily dreams show that the dreamer has multiple conceptions which cannot and should not be reduced to a single unitary idea. A dreamer may conceive of his mother as generous, protective, amorous, mean, forbidding, punishing, unreliable, jealous and distant.

These various conceptions are called a conceptual system since they are ideas that relate to a single object, in this case, the mother. Conceptions may be logically contradictory because logic does not guide the mental operations of a dreamer. He is free to view the world in as many ways as his mind takes him. The task of the interpreter is to follow the dreams of a series wherever they may lead and not to impose unity of conception where no unity exists. The mind of man is a complicated system which does not lend itself to easy simplification.

It is recommended, however, that one try to understand why a person can harbor contradictory notions. Why, for example, can he conceive of his mother as both punishing and protective. The answer will often be found in the circumstances in which each conception is embedded. For instance, in one dream the mother may appear as protective because the dreamer is in danger, and in another dream as punishing because the dreamer has rebelled against her authority. Each conception is consistent with the context of the whole dream.

This brings us to a fourth rule. It should be borne in mind that a dream is an organic whole; one part of a dream should not be lifted out of context and interpreted for itself alone. The dream should be interpreted as a whole, because it reflects an interconnected network of ideas in the mind of the dreamer. I would go even further and say that a dream ought never to be analyzed for its meaning without consulting other dreams of a series in order to see how the thoughts of a person are tied together. By analyzing a dream series one arrives at a more comprehensive and more coherent view of the conceptual systems of a person.

In any discussion of dream interpretation the question of dream symbols and how they are to be translated is bound to arise. This question is such a complex one that it will require a chapter to itself. To the subject of dream symbols we now turn.

5   Why There Are Symbols in Dreams

IT IS a very old notion that dreams make use of a secret language which must be mastered before a dream can be properly understood. In ancient times only a few people knew this language and they were highly esteemed as dream interpreters. Ultimately someone wrote down this secret language in a book so that it was made available to everyone. The person who did this was an Italian scholar, Artemidorus, who lived in the second century of the Christian era. He called his book *Oneirocritics*, which means the art of interpreting dreams. Following the invention of the printing press in the fifteenth century *Oneirocritics* was translated into many tongues and appeared in numerous editions. It was an extremely popular book, this Adam of all dream books, and as might be expected stimulated the publication of other dream books, many of which drew freely upon the scholarship of Artemidorus. The first American dream book, *The Book of Knowledge,* was published in Boston in 1767 and was followed by many others. Today a wide selection of dream books is available to anyone who wants help in interpreting his dreams.

A dream book is like a dictionary. It contains a list of words or phrases, alphabetically arranged, and each of these items is followed by an explanation. The word or phrase describes something that has occurred in a dream while the explanation is the meaning of this dream item. For example, if one dreams of taking a journey, he looks up "journey" in a dream book and finds that a journey signifies death. In other words he has had a prophetic dream of his own death. A dream book makes it possible for anyone to decode his own dreams without the help of an expert. Although serious students of dreams do not place any confidence in dream books, the notion that dreams employ a secret language of symbols persists in modern scientific writings. Freud, who possessed the most profound and penetrating mind of anyone who has studied dreams, believed that symbols appear in dreams and tried to show why this should be true. His argument went as follows. During sleep the mind thinks about things that would be abhorrent to the person when he is awake. If he were awake, he would drive them out of awareness lest they should drive him out of his mind. Even during sleep, however, a person will not tolerate the expression of certain ideas in a crude form; they have to be smuggled into dreams by being transformed into innocuous symbols. A symbol Freud believed is a disguise for a reprehensible thought. One dreams of climbing a tree instead of masturbating because climbing trees is condoned while masturbating is condemned.

Since Freud thought that dreams were motivated largely by sex, his dream symbols are preponderantly disguises for sexual things, such as the male and female genitals, intercourse and masturbation. Consider the following dream of a young woman from this point of view.

I was in a big room talking to one of my friends. She said she was going riding and I decided to join her. I waited for her to come back for me; when she did return, she said she had already plowed the field and that the horse was upstairs. I said that I'd probably have trouble getting it down the stairs, and she told me one of the men had helped her down. However, I decided against riding. Later, we were all sitting around in the room and I looked up and saw a friend of mine who was in New Orleans. He came over and we were talking until everyone was handed an enormous gun and we all started shooting out of the windows. I recall loading and reloading the gun.

In the dream language of psychoanalysis this dream is a versatile portrayal of sexuality. Riding a horse, plowing a field, climbing stairs and shooting a gun symbolize sexual intercourse. Gun, horse and plow stand for the male member while room and window represent the female sex organs. The fact that the dreamer is given an enormous gun with which she shoots out of the window means that she wants to have the sexual equipment of a male. According to Freud, many women want to be men.

Why does plowing a field represent sexual intercourse? Why does a gun stand for the penis and a window for the vagina? How does a symbol get to be a symbol? The stock answer of psychoanalysis to this question is that a symbol becomes a symbol because it resembles that which it stands for. A plow, for example, penetrates the earth just as a penis penetrates the vagina. Riding a horse involves the same up and down movement of two bodies as in a sexual embrace. Climbing stairs expresses the mounting desire of sexual ardor. A gun resembles a penis both in shape and function, and a window is like a vagina because it is an opening into a large structure.

In a psychoanalytic dream book one learns that all circular objects and containers symbolize the vagina and all oblong objects symbolize the penis because of a resemblance in shape. All objects that emit something, for example, a fountain pen or a syringe, stand for the male organ, which has the same function. Color resemblances provide other symbols, chocolate for feces, yellow for urine, and milk for semen. Similarity in value explains why jewelry can be a substitute for the female genitals and similarity in quality accounts for the use of wild animals as symbols of sexual passion.

In addition to resemblance psychoanalysis places considerable emphasis upon the principle of contrast in the formation of symbols. To dream of being in a crowd means that one is alone, to dream of being clothed means that one is naked, and to dream of dying means that one is alive. The notion that dreams go by contraries is one of the oldest maxims of dream lore as well as one of the pillars of psychoanalytic dream interpretation.

I have no fault to find with the idea that a dreamer uses symbols in his dreams just as he uses symbols in waking life. What I do object to is Freud's theory of dream symbolism which states that symbols serve to hide something obnoxious. My objection is based upon a number of considerations. In the first place, a dreamer may have a disguised dream of an incestuous relationship one night and a perfectly barefaced dream of incest the next night. As Jocasta says to Oedipus, "Many young men dream of sleeping with their mothers." What is the sense of preparing an elaborate disguise in one dream when it is discarded in another dream? I have not been able to find a convincing answer to this question in Freudian theory.

Then there is the fact that many people are able to translate their dreams although they have no acquaintance with psychoanalysis. What good does it do to disguise something in a dream when the person is able to see through the disguise when he wakes up? Freud does not answer this question.

A third objection to Freud's disguise theory is found in the widespread use of slang in waking life. There are many slang expressions for sexual anatomy and sexual activities. Some of these slang words are identical with those found in a psychoanalytic dream book. Since the meaning of slang is known to those who use it, how can these expressions be employed to hide one's true thoughts in dreams? For instance, gun, pistol and cannon are slang expressions for penis and they are also recognized as dream symbols for the same organ. Is it likely that a gun would appear in a dream in order to fool the dreamer when he uses gun or some variation of it as a slang expression for the male genital organ in waking life? I do not think so.

Finally we raise a question that has not been given proper attention by those who believe that a symbol hides something.

Why are there so many symbols for the same referent? In a search of the literature we found one hundred and two different dream symbols for penis, ninety-five for vagina and fifty-five for sexual intercourse. Is it necessary to hide these reprehensible referents behind such a vast array of masks? Or do these multitudes of synonyms signify something quite different about the meaning of symbols in dreams?

At this point the reader has a right to ask, "If you are so discontented with Freud's explanation for why there are symbols in dreams, why don't you suggest a better explanation?" This is exactly what we intend to do. We believe there are symbols in dreams and that these symbols serve a necessary function, but it is not the function of disguise. We believe that the symbols of dreams are there to express something, not to hide it.

In order to develop this thesis clearly and systematically, let us repeat what we have already said about dreaming. Dreaming is a form of thinking and thinking consists of formulating conceptions or ideas. When one dreams, his conceptions are turned into pictures. The images of a dream are the concrete embodiments of the dreamer's thoughts; these images give visible expression to that which is invisible, namely, conceptions.

Accordingly the true referent of any dream symbol is not an object or activity, it is always an idea in the mind of a dreamer. A visible object, gun, does not stand for another visible object, penis; rather it may stand for the dreamer's idea of penis, if he conceives of the penis as a dangerous weapon. Of course, gun may not represent a sexual conception at all but signify

some non-sexual idea in the dreamer's thoughts. A little later
we will try to explain how one can discover the real referent
of any dream symbol.

Suppose that a person dreams about a cow and that it is discovered that cow expresses the dreamer's conception of his
mother. Why does he find it necessary to symbolize his idea
of his mother in this manner? Our reply is that he wants to
express as clearly and as economically as possible the feeling
that his mother is a nurturant person. He probably has many
other ideas about his mother but in this dream he wants to
focus on a single quality, her nurturance, so he selects a symbol,
cow, which embodies this particular quality. Why doesn't he
just dream about his mother doing nurturant things, for instance, waiting on him, serving him a meal, or taking care of
him, instead of transforming her into a cow? Our answer is
that an image of a cow is such an easy and direct way of representing what he feels. It is a kind of mental shorthand—
"My mother is a cowlike person, ergo let her appear as a cow
in my dream." In waking life, symbols are used for precisely
the same reason. A lion stands for courage, a snake for evil
and an owl for wisdom. Likewise, a cross stands for the Christian church, John Bull for England and a hammer and sickle
for Soviet Russia. These symbols convey in terse and concise
language complex and abstruse conceptions.

Obviously, one's idea of the symbol must be identical with
his idea of the referent. That is, if cow is going to stand for
mother, the dreamer's conception of cow has to be congruent
with his conception of mother. The idea of a cow as a nurturant beast equals the idea of a mother as a nurturant person.

If the dreamer conceived of cows as dangerous animals he could hardly choose a cow as a symbol of his mother conception.

This viewpoint regarding symbols explains why there are apparently so many different symbols for the same thing. Actually the same thing is not being represented in various ways, but different conceptions of the same thing require different symbols. Thus one conception of sexual intercourse is that it is a generative or reproductive activity. Such a conception finds appropriate visible representation in the plowing of a field or the planting of seeds. Another conception of sexual intercourse is that it is an aggressive physical attack, in which case one might dream of shooting a person with a gun, stabbing someone with a dagger, or running someone down with an automobile.

Sometimes a symbol is chosen because it represents in a single object a variety of conceptions. The moon may be regarded as a condensed symbol of woman. The monthly phases of the moon resemble the menstrual cycle, a resemblance that has support from etymology since the words moon and menses are derived from the same Latin word. The filling out of the moon from new to full simulates the rounding out of the woman during pregnancy. The moon is inferior to the sun, a male symbol. The moon is changeable like a fickle woman while the sun is constant. The moon sheds a weak light which embodies the idea of feminine frailty. The moon controls the ebb and flow of the tides, another likeness to the female rhythm. Rhythm, change, fruitfulness, weakness and submissiveness, all of these conventional conceptions of woman are compressed into a single visible object.

There is no getting around it, the presence of symbols in dreams makes the difficult task of extracting meaning from dreams even more difficult. If one dreamed only of the things themselves one could discover the dreamer's conceptions of these objects by observing the context in which they appear. That is, if one dreamed of his mother performing nurturant acts it would be pretty apparent that he conceived of his mother as a nurturant person. However, if she appears as a cow it is necessary to decipher cow into mother and then, in addition, determine the dreamer's conception of cows in order to determine his conception of mother.

What rules and procedures should be followed in locating and deciphering dream symbols? One pretty reliable rule to follow is that if the dream does not make sense taken at its face value one should look for a symbol which when appropriately translated will make the dream sensible. The following dream reported by a young woman may be used to illustrate this rule.

I was riding a horse with a saddle, and everything was fine. All of a sudden the saddle and reins fell off except for one rein. The horse was a large powerful horse. The horse told me that he was going to try and throw me off. I told him that I would stay on no matter what happened. The horse kicked and ran between trees as fast as he could. I stayed on him and then woke up.

The presence of a symbol is suggested by a horse which talks. A person may talk to a horse but a horse, save in fairy tales, cannot talk back. In order to make the dream sensible horse is translated into human being. Since the horse is referred to by the masculine pronoun, the human being is assumed to be a male. The description of the horse as large and powerful suggests that the male is an adult. Accordingly the dream reveals the dreamer's conception of her relationship with a man. At the beginning of the dream their relationship is a satisfactory one as seen by the dreamer. She is sitting securely in the saddle and everything is fine. Then her conception of their relationship takes a turn for the worse. The saddle and one rein fall off and she is left clutching precariously the other rein. The horse and the dreamer pit their skill against each other, the rider trying to stay on while the horse tries to throw her off. Victory finally goes to the dreamer. What she is saying in this dream is that she thinks a man with whom she has an intimate association is trying to get rid of her. Who could the man be? It might be either her father, her brother or her boy friend. Which one of these three it is cannot be determined from this dream alone. However, it might be learned by consulting other dreams of this girl, by asking her if she has any idea who the horse could be, or by getting her to say what comes into her mind when she thinks of horses.

Let us consider each of these methods in turn. A young woman dreamed that it was her first wedding anniversary and she and her husband were going to re-enact the ceremony. She could not find her wedding gown and searched for it frantically.

Finally when I found the gown, it was dirty and torn. With tears of disappointment in my eyes I snatched the gown and hurried to the church. Upon my arrival my husband inquired why I had brought the gown with me. I was confused and bewildered and felt strange and alone.

Suppose we assume that the state of her wedding dress symbolizes the dreamer's conception of her marriage. What evidence can be found in her other dreams to support such an interpretation? She dreams about a recently married girl who is getting a divorce, which suggests that the idea of divorce is in the dreamer's mind even though she attributes it to one of her friends. In another dream she has a difficult time trying to get home to her husband. She loses her way, falls on the sidewalk, is delayed by a train, and never does reach her destination. This dream suggests that she is trying to find reasons for not returning home to her husband. She dreams that the diamond in her engagement ring is missing hoping perhaps that this would nullify her unhappy marriage. Finally, she dreams that her girl friend who is getting married receives a lot of useless wedding presents. The state of marriage she thinks is like so much useless truck.

Surely these dreams indicate that the dreamer conceives of her marriage as an unhappy one and corroborate the hypothesis that her torn and dirty wedding dress is a concrete embodiment of this idea. By this time it should be pretty obvious to the reader that the interpretation of dreams is made much easier when one has a series of dreams to work with rather than having to depend upon single dreams.

Occasionally it is possible to learn from the dreamer himself what a particular symbol stands for by asking him. This procedure is illustrated in the case of a young man who dreamed that he was trying to persuade a native to help him escape from a camp. The dreamer had a furlough coming to him but his commanding officer would not let him take it.

The native couldn't speak English but he made me understand by manipulating a ladderlike, brown, wooden object.

In commenting upon this dream the young man said, "For some reason or other, the object the native manipulated reminded me of a man. The two long legs were the legs of a man and the cross piece was his genital organs." With this piece of information the dream can be given a plausible interpretation. The commanding officer and the army camp stand for discipline from which a furlough would come as a welcome relief. The native signifies the dreamer's impulses, which express themselves by means of a concrete sexual activity, namely, manipulation of the genitals. In short, this dream symbolizes the young man's conception of sexual gratification through masturbation.

An even better method for securing information about symbols is to ask a person to say everything that comes into his mind when he thinks about something that has appeared or occurred in a dream. This is the famous free association method developed by Freud and used by psychoanalysts throughout the world to plumb the depths of the unconscious mind.

In free associating to a dream one free associates to each phrase or sentence in the dream in turn, and then reconstructs the meaning of the whole dream from the separate associations. The following dream reported by a young man exemplifies this method of getting at the meaning of dream symbols.

I was at a gas station where I work and my friend Bob was there also working. It seemed to me that he was new and inexperienced at the job, because I was watching him check the oil on a car. He pulled out the oil dipstick and looked at it. At this point I went up to him rather angrily and said, "Bob, in order to check the oil you have to wipe off the oil on the dipstick first and then put the dipstick back in, pull it out and then get a reading." He thanked me for my help and the dream ended.

When asked to say what came into his mind when he thought of checking oil, the dreamer said it reminded him of sexual intercourse, and that Bob was not doing it properly. He then went on to say that Bob went around with prostitutes which the dreamer felt was wrong and he wished that Bob would quit doing it. The action of inserting the dipstick into the oil hole is a direct representation of intercourse and reveals a pretty mechanical conception of sexual gratification.

Another young man dreamed that after playing a long and difficult piano selection of his own composition he went over to the conductor of the orchestra and kissed his hand. His associations to conductor were as follows:

Conductor-leader-person-of-authority-my father. I am extremely grateful to father for developing my talents. If my father wasn't behind me I couldn't do things. When I was a young child I resented him making me play the piano but today I'm most grateful to him.

The dreamer's conceptions of his father as a guide, leader and authority are condensed into a single personification, the orchestra conductor.

A different conception of a father is portrayed in the dream of another young man. This is the dream.

I had reported for class at the university and saw that my instructor was the same man who is now training me on a new job. He reprimanded me for failing to pay attention. The scene shifted to a cafeteria where this same instructor was studying at a table with a friend of mine. I was afraid to approach because of what had happened previously but the instructor did not look up so I walked up to him anyway. I began copying calculus answers from my friend.

To instructor, the dreamer gave the following associations.

Instructor is man who is training me on job. He was my friend before I got the job. He's an ardent Catholic who believes in hard and fast rules as far as religion is concerned but does not always follow these rules himself. He represents figure of my father in capacity of teaching and instructing. Has same tendency of neglecting subjective feeling side of situation as my father has. My father always wanted to show me, didn't let me do it. Gave me feeling of incompetence by doing it himself.

Notice how the dreamer himself recognizes that he uses instructor to represent one aspect of his father, namely, his role as a teacher. He then goes on in his associations to give a more complete picture of his father.

Dad is a funny sort of fellow. Very practical, old-school type of person. Keeps his emotions repressed, yet at home he was punishing agent. It was Dad whom you feared. After my mother died I had an idea that my father would never get married again. Yet he married my stepmother whom we all dislike, but I dislike intensely. I felt he was not living up to my standards. Never thought he could get married or wished he would not get married. He did not live up to what I thought were his standards.

The dreamer is afraid to approach the instructor because as he says,

Father never was object of affection, only fear. Am always afraid to approach him on any problem. He's ignoring me. Not deeply concerned, distant, rejecting me. I'm sitting with him, meaning living with him, yet not able to approach him on any problem.

About the copying, the dreamer says,

I had taken calculus previously at another school. It was an obligation to my father because he wanted me to take it. I'm fulfilling obligation of calculus to my father, yet in fulfilling it there is an element of deceit.

These associations, all of which were touched off by the presence of an instructor in his dream show plainly what the dreamer thinks about his father. His father is an insensitive person who does not let his son learn by doing but has to show him so that the boy feels incompetent. The dreamer hates and fears his father, hates him because he married again and fears him because he is a threatening person. Because he feels this way the son cannot seek his father's help. He submits to his father but his submission is really a subterfuge.

In another case a dreamer's conception of his status as a male is symbolized in the dream action of getting on a very small railroad handcar no larger than a toy and pumping furiously. The tiny handcar, according to his associations, represents his idea of his penis, which he feels is very small. Pumping furiously signifies masturbation, which he says is his only sexual outlet.

Numerous other examples of the deciphering of symbols by free association could be given but the foregoing ones are sufficient to illustrate the usefulness of this method. Anyone can free associate if he is able and willing to let his mind go and not try to control, edit and suppress what appears in the stream of consciousness. It is done best when one is relaxed and away from all external distractions, preferably while lying on a bed or couch in a quiet room. He should then let the images of a dream come into his mind one at a time and see what he associates with each image before going to the next one. In this way almost any unusual or difficult feature of a dream will yield its secret.

We would emphasize again, however, that many dreams can be properly interpreted without recourse to free associations since their meaning is transparent. Is it necessary to do any decoding of the following dream?

I dreamed that my unit head at camp had been doing little mean things to me. She seemed to exclude me from her conversation, to comment only when my work was unsatisfactory and to reprimand me in front of others. I was extremely unhappy. I felt that I could not tell of my unhappines to anyone, not even to my husband. Somehow I had the feeling that no one would understand me.

Doesn't this dream give us a pretty clear idea of the dreamer's conception of an older woman, of her husband and of her life predicament in general? We might obtain much fuller information about what is preying on her mind if we had her associations to this dream. We might find that the unit head treats her as she feels her mother treats her, but would this information really add very much to what we already know from the dream itself?

Would associations contribute anything to our understanding of this dream?

My girl and I were skiing down a long bushy slope. We were holding hands, then I fell and she fell over me into a big powdery drift. We sat up laughing, snow up to our necks. I kissed her and when I opened my eyes we were in a log cabin sitting before a fire. We smiled at each other. "You said this would be nice. It's wonderful," she said. "Mmmmmuuuuummmmmmm," I replied.

Perhaps free association would add little sexual nuances to skiing down a bushy slope, falling into a snow drift, and sitting before a fire in a log cabin, but the sensual quality of the dream is there already and does not need to be supplemented by associations.

Even the next dream, which contains some symbolism, is not hard to understand if one is willing to make a single assumption.

I was the warden at a very inefficient prison for criminals. All at once the gates to the prison opened and all the criminals tried to escape. They tried to beat me up and trample on me and I was left standing there completely helpless.

If one grants that the criminals in this dream symbolize the dreamer's conception of her own impulses, then the translation of the dream follows directly. The dreamer is trying to hold her impulses in check but she is not equal to the task. They break out, assault her, and leave her with a feeling of helplessness. This dream tells us that the young woman conceives of her impulses as lawless, destructive forces against which reason and conscience are powerless.

When a dream does not divulge its meaning readily, we can usually discover its meaning by consulting other dreams of the same person. The method of analyzing dreams by series rather than in isolation is always to be preferred.

In concluding this chapter on dream symbols let us return to the question of dream books with which this chapter began. Dream books were written specifically to help people understand and profit from their dreams. They first appeared when people quite generally believed that dreams contained omens of the future. These omens might be good or bad, but in either case, the omen always appeared disguised in a symbol. The Pharaoh's dream of seven fat cattle and seven lean cattle which Joseph interpreted is a prototype of the symbolically represented omen. Because Joseph interpreted the king's dream correctly, appropriate measures were taken to forestall the seven years of famine by stockpiling food during the seven bountiful years.

Today there are many people who believe in dream omens and who regularly consult dream books in order to foretell the future. As we have said before this practice has no scientific justification. On the other hand, there are scientific dream books which do not subscribe to the notion of omens but which purport to help a person decipher the symbols in his dreams.

What is the status of these modern counterparts of Artemidorus's *Oneirocritics*? We believe that they can be depended upon as little as the old-style dream book. The language of dream symbols is an individual language not a universal one as these modern dream books would have us believe. Each dreamer uses a different symbolic language from every other dreamer because no two people have exactly the same conceptual systems and therefore no two people can share the same dream language. Dream symbols are private, personal emblems of thought and cannot be codified in the form of a dictionary. There may be a few symbols that are shared by a number of people but even these are probably not timeless or universal in meaning. That is why we caution against the mechanical interpretation of dreams by using dream books, whether of the old style or new. Let the dream or dream series say what it has to say without trying to force a meaning on it from some outside source.

Why then are there symbols in dreams? There are symbols in dreams for the same reason that there are figures of speech in poetry and slang in everyday life. Man wants to express his thoughts as clearly as possible in objective terms. He wants to convey meaning with precision and economy. He wants to clothe his conceptions in the most appropriate garments. And perhaps, although of this we are not too certain, he wants to garnish his ideas with beauty and taste. For these reasons the language of sleep uses symbols.

6   The Human Triangle

OUR PERIOD of history has been called the age of anxiety for reasons that seem self-evident to thoughtful men. Yet when we stop to consider man's past as reflected in literature, art, history and social institutions we find that this quality of apprehension does not distinguish our age from any other age. For man is and always has been the anxious animal. Anxiety seems to be a basic condition of human existence and a powerful motivating force in shaping individual and group enterprises. The atom bomb, for example, is a product of man's fear rather than a cause of it, as so many people seem to think. Until we learn this lesson all attempts to solve the problem of war or other social ills will be abortive ones.

Man is the anxious animal because he suffers from inner conflict. His personality is a house divided against itself and civil war is its natural state. The consequence of inner strife is mental torment, which impels man to act in ways that will relieve his suffering, little realizing that his actions rarely come to grips with the reasons for his anxiety. For he looks out toward the world to resolve his inner tensions when he should look inward to discover and eliminate the roots of his anxiety.

What are these conflicts which breed anxiety? Because they are apt to be lodged in the deeper recesses of man's mind, it is necessary to use special tools analogous to the X-ray to bring them to light. Dreams are such a tool, for dreams are a record of the subjective side of human existence. When the mind is cut off from the external world it turns in upon itself and dwells upon its own problems and perplexities. These nocturnal thoughts issue forth as dreams to provide a record of the ambiguities which assail man.

With this in mind we have gone to our large collection of dreams gathered from people who are essentially normal to seek an answer to the question, What are the inner conflicts of man? We have not approached this study with preconceived ideas of what we want to find. Rather we have let our collection of dreams speak for itself and tell us what is in man's mind. In the following chapters we propose to discuss some of the major conflicts that are bodied forth in dreams.

We have named the first conflict, the human triangle, because it involves the relationship among three people, the dreamer and two others. It will be recalled that the average number of dream characters including the dreamer is a threesome. The particular triangle we have in mind consists of the dreamer and a man and a woman. If the dreamer is a man, the threesome is two men and a woman, if the dreamer is a woman, the threesome is two women and a man. Such triangles are commonplace in life and fiction and usually take the form of two men competing for a woman or two women competing for a man. Is it not astonishing that people are willing to expose themselves to the constant reiteration of this theme in movies, plays and novels? They never seem to tire of it, not even in their dreams.

The reason why the theme of the human triangle never loses its appeal is that it reflects a significant internal conflict which maintains a stubborn hold over the minds of men. In such cases, we obtain some vicarious relief by seeing it resolved for us in the fantasies of movies, plays and novels. Likewise we look for solutions in our own nocturnal imaginings.

Let us be more explicit about the nature of this triangle as it is found in dreams. In the dreams of men the typical pattern is one in which the dreamer conceives of another man as a dangerous rival for the love of a woman. The dreamer employs many strategies to outwit his rival and possess the object of his desire. In the dreams of women the situation is the same except that the dreamer's rival is another woman and the object they are competing for is a man.

This conflict is one of long standing in the life of every person going back to the earliest of all threesome relationships, the child and his parents. Very early in life a boy comes to view his father as a rival for the mother's affection while a girl sees her mother as a competitor for the father's love. In the family setting as elsewhere two's company, three's a crowd.

The reality of this family triangle and the person's contrasting conception of his father and mother are clearly portrayed in dreams. The frankness of dreams is sometimes appalling, as is the case with the following dreams in which a person's longing for the parent of opposite sex is explicitly and crudely represented.

I dreamed I was having intercourse with my mother. She was fully dressed as was I, and I attempted to have intercourse while standing by simple friction of my penis while embracing her passionately.

I dreamed I was married to a much older man who was short and fat. We were standing in a house at a big window looking out. Outside were many people who seemed to be protesting against my relationship with this man. We were calmly watching these people, who seemed to be my close friends, and I seemed perfectly satisfied and contented with this older man, who resembled my father.

In both of these dreams the dreamer is not without a sense of guilt. This is indicated in the first dream by the boy and his mother being fully clothed and in the second dream by the people who are protesting against the marriage.

Hostility toward the parent of the same sex is the theme of the next two dreams, the first one reported by a man and the second one by a young woman.

I dreamed I was standing on the stairs dueling with swords with my father. I ran him through the shoulder and then stood over him yelling and crying.

I dreamed my mother said something to me that suggested I had been having an affair with Jim. I got perfectly, wildly furious, all the more angry because I knew I had been considering it. I was beside myself and yet incapable of expressing it. I couldn't scream and I seemed paralyzed. It was terrible and was getting worse when I woke up.

The second dream is more complex than the first one since it displays not only the dreamer's resentment against her mother but also presents the reason for her anger. She hates her mother because her mother suggests that the dreamer is having an affair with a boy friend. The mother in this case is a personification of the dreamer's conscience.

We took a large number of dreams in which one or both parents appeared and divided them according to whether there was friendliness or hostility between the dreamer and his mother and father. In the dreams of men the relationship with the mother is usually portrayed as being friendly while the relationship with the father is typically unfriendly. In women just the reverse is true—positive feelings for the father and negative feelings for the mother being the trend. If we take all older characters in dreams instead of just parents, practically the same results are found. Men conceive of older men as enemies and of older women as friends while women conceive of older men as friends and of older women as enemies. Apparently the image one has of his parents determines how he will see all older people.

It is an interesting fact that women do not divide their parents into friendly fathers and hostile mothers as sharply as men divide their parents into hostile fathers and friendly mothers. Women are more apt than men to have mixed feelings about each parent. This difference between men and women is not surprising when one considers the origin of these particular conceptions. Babies of either sex develop a warm positive feeling for the mother and regard the father as an interloper. Later a girl under the influence of frustrations imposed by the mother and a more or less active wooing by the father shifts her affection from mother to father. Still a residue of the girl's earlier conceptions remains so that she is more mixed up than the boy, whose conceptions of the father and mother do not undergo such a marked reversal. Consequently women tend to have more trouble in their personal relationships than men do because their conceptions of parents are more vacillating.

The ambiguous feelings of a young woman for her parents is strikingly depicted in the following dream.

I dreamed I was in a lake with my mother and father. It was getting dark. The water was covered with a film like oil would produce. At first we were all swimming out from shore in this filmed area, father on my left, mother on my right. Then the filmy area separated. My father remained in the large filmy area, my mother in the smaller one, while I was left in clear water. I wanted to swim toward my father but I was told or somehow received the feeling that he was not worth swimming to, that he was not good, so I swam toward my mother. Just as I entered the filmy part she was in, I got the feeling that my father was really O.K. but that we had misunderstood him. It was too late, however, to try to go to him so I kept on swimming toward my mother.

In dreams we see not only the conflicts that arise out of parent-child relationships but we are also told how the dreamer attempts to resolve these conflicts in his imagination. Dreams contain a number of ingenious plots for reaching desired goals. Here, for example, is a dream that contains a clever ruse by which the dreamer gets her father to make love to her.

Mother, Dad and I were driving along in the car. Mom was driving and Dad had his arm around me. We began discussing the old and new ways of making love and I wondered if the fellows used to use a different technique than they do now. Dad said he would show me and then started to make love to me. I was very shocked but he and Mom didn't seem to think anything of it.

Although the plan is a clever one the dreamer does not evade completely the voice of conscience, for she is shocked by her father's behavior, which means that she is shocked by the fulfillment of her own wish that her father should make love to her. She feels guilty even though she has her mother and father appear unconcerned by this incestuous love-making.

In other dreams reported by this same woman her antagonism toward the mother manifests itself. She has her mother grow old and helpless following a tooth extraction in one dream.

My grandfather had his dentist's coat on and had just pulled one of Mother's back teeth. When I saw her it was a great shock because her hair was all white and my mother actually has pure brown hair. She looked so old and helpless. I was frightened and began to cry.

In another dream she is able to express her aggression more openly by substituting an unfamiliar older woman for the mother.

Suddenly the old woman gasped and fell on the floor in pain saying she had a heart attack. I was sitting on a chair and yet I was watching myself stroking the woman's neck. I was saying,

"Why don't I choke her to death and get out of this terrible mess?" Just then the woman died and thunderous music got louder and louder.

Here she actually kills the older woman in order to get out of the terrible mess created by her inner conflict. In other words she could have her father's love completely if only her mother could be put out of the way.

Where there is hate there is usually fear, so it comes as no surprise to find that this dreamer fears her mother. The following dream represents her fear of an older woman.

My roommate and I were sitting on a high wall overlooking a roaring ocean. There was a small beach below the wall with many huts scattered along it. There was one hut that we kept close watch of and every time a woman, about sixty years old, would come out of it we had to duck in the bushes to avoid her seeing us. I don't remember what our reason was for being afraid of her. Then we walked toward a large mansion which was about fifty feet from the wall with a glassed-in porch overlooking the ocean.

Although this dream does not divulge the reason for her fear we might guess that it has something to do with the public display of love-making which she carried on with her father in an earlier dream. This guess is borne out by a dream in which she openly exhibits her naked body.

I unbuttoned my coat and was horrified to discover I didn't have any clothes on. I was carrying them on my arm. The bus came and I had to sit next to a prudish old woman who was shocked at my condition. My coat just wouldn't stay around me and I was the laughingstock of the bus. I was red with embarrassment and humiliation.

The prudish old woman is the dreamer's conception of her mother, the thought of whom makes the dreamer feel very ashamed.

The conflicting conceptions of the dreamer are embodied in this cycle of dreams. She wants her father to love her sensually but she feels guilty when he does. She hates her mother enough to want to kill her yet she is afraid of her mother. Actually it is her own conscience that she fears.

A young man's conflict between an incestuous wish and a fear of the father's revenge is presented in the following two-part dream.

I was lying awake and a tall dark woman came to my bed dressed in a long black velvet gown with a zipper up the front. She began to kiss me and make love to me and got in bed with me. Just then a woman of whom I am very fond appeared and the whole dream vanished.

Next I found myself in a castle or large house in Mexico or Spain. There were two men, one younger and the other older, struggling with each other. At last both of them secured weapons, broad flat swords like Turkish scimitars and the fight continued. The younger man was badly wounded in the abdomen; there was much blood. He seemed to die. Suddenly he was all right again. He was forgiven by the older man. Everything was very pleasant, and the whole affair ended on a happy note.

The second part of the dream is the punishment and atonement for the erotic gratification with a mother figure in the first part. The older man is the dreamer's father, the younger man is the dreamer himself. They fight, the son is mortally wounded, dies, comes to life, and is forgiven by the father. Having expiated his sin, the dreamer is received back into the good graces of the father. Thus the conflict is resolved.

Another solution is offered in this young man's dream. He kills a father figure and is protected from the police by his mother.

When the dream began I had just returned from some place and was in a house. I was trying to decide how to kill a man, about forty years old. The next feeling I had was that I had killed this person. Then the phone rang and I answered it. The party at the other end asked for "Joseph" and I in some way let him know that Joseph was dead. Then a feeling of complete helplessness came over me. The next scene was where my mother and I were waiting at the front door of our home for the police to come. A siren sounded and a police car pulled into the drive. I left the scene and when I came back the police had left and my mother said she had told them I was not at home. Here I woke up.

Here, as in other dreams, the dreamer is overwhelmed by a sense of guilt for having given way to a murderous impulse and is made to feel helpless by his conscience, which appears in the form of police officers. Fortunately his conception of his mother is such that she is able to save him.

Another version of the conflict between love and shame is set forth in this woman's dream.

In this dream my roommate's father fell in love with me. Her parents came up to school from New York and I had never met them before this dream. I felt very badly about the situation as my roommate blamed me and her mother was heartbroken.

The father and mother of her roommate stand in place of her parents, a transformation which serves to allay her shame. She cannot bring herself to think of marrying her own father even in fantasy but it is permissible for her to steal her roommate's father away from his wife. In spite of this subterfuge she feels guilty for what she has done.

Another strategy employed by dreamers is to attribute the sexual longing which really exists in the mind of the dreamer to the parent of opposite sex. "I love him" is transformed into "He loves me," following which the dreamer becomes afraid when the parent makes advances. This is the motivation for the following dream of a young woman.

My father was trying to get in my apartment so I ran to the front door and locked it. He then started to climb over the porch railing and I frantically locked the porch door. I felt that I had to escape so I unlocked the front room windows which are out of line with the porch windows and tried to let myself out. There is a drop of about twenty feet to the ground and I felt that I could lower myself gradually the length of my arms and then drop the rest of the way. I woke up then, terribly frightened, my hands were wet from perspiration and I was all excited and it took me a while to get back to sleep.

There is no reason why she should be so afraid of her own father. Her frantic efforts to keep him out of her apartment, her terrifying panic, and the excitement that persists even after she awakens are responses to an inner wish to be seduced by the father.

Strong ties of affection between child and parent often make it difficult for the child to establish a love relationship outside of the family. When a young man or woman falls in love, he may feel like a traitor to his mother or father. Parents are known to reinforce this feeling by openly resenting their children's boy friends and girl friends. Many a young person has had to face parental disapproval when he makes known his plans to get married.

The guilt felt by a girl of twenty who dreams she is getting married is reflected in this dream.

I dreamed I wished to be married and everyone was happy about the ceremony except me. Although I wanted to be married I felt I was going against something or somebody. I felt guilty. Then suddenly my father tried to choke me to death. He was very composed. He showed no emotion while choking me. I wasn't afraid of death but of my father. To be a little clearer I was more afraid of having made my father angry than of being killed myself.

The dreamer feels that she is acting contrary to her father's wishes and that he has a right to punish her for being unfaithful. Whether the father actually feels this way or not is irrelevant since it is the dreamer's guilt, not the father's attitude, which motivates the dream.

The state of indecision during which a young person fluctuates between remaining faithful to the beloved parent and transferring her affection to someone outside the family circle is mirrored in this dream of a young woman.

I dreamed I was lying on a bed with a man and we were making very passionate love, and yet sexual intercourse was not carried on. The man resembled my father one instant, and the next he resembled my fiancé.

She manages to have her father and her fiancé simultaneously, a highly improbable yet very satisfying solution to her conflict.

In another dream reported by this same person she chooses her father.

I dreamed I was married to my father. We had not been married very long and we were engaged in some sort of restaurant business. There were a lot of people mingled through the dream who were evidently weekend guests. I recognized two of the people as my brother and grandfather. My father and I were very happy in marriage and he was very understanding toward my adjustment to it.

Numerous complications arise in the lives of young people which make it more difficult to break through the family triangle. For example, a young man who had fallen in love with a girl was unwilling to desert his mother because he thought his father was such a mean, inadequate person and that it was his duty to protect and provide for his mother. It is this conflict which he tries to solve in his dreams.

He fancies that his girl will help him out of his difficulties in these two dreams.

I dreamed that I left my house in order to do my homework at my girl's house. She was helping me through a tough situation at home. She changed the subject and made me think of the work I had to do.

I dreamed that I had a time struggling for existence and my wife [actually his girl friend] stood by and encouraged me and never let me down.

However, this solution is not satisfactory since it leaves his mother out of consideration as the following dream shows.

I dreamed that my mother was crying. I had the feeling that she was hurt. I tried to comfort her but it was no use.

If he marries his girl, his mother will be left alone. With this on his mind he decides, in the next dream, to renounce marriage.

My girl friend pled with me to marry her and she would go to work so I could be away from home and do good college work. She cried and I intended to leave her because I can't stand anybody crying. I was thinking about what my mother and we kids went through and I was debating with myself if I had the right to entertain any ideas of marriage.

Not satisfied with this solution, he comes up with one in the next dream which seems to take care of everything.

I dreamed I bought my mother two pretty dresses and a lovely fur coat. My father had died, I was married and we were living in a dwelling that my mother had always wanted. My mother and wife got along beautifully and on occasions I complimented my wife for her cooking and she would reply that it was only possible because of my mother. I think I also dreamed something about a baby but that is vague.

He gets rid of his father, marries his girl and has his mother live with them. The only trouble with this dream is that it is completely unrealistic. The dreamer, living in the shadow of an inadequate father, has no confidence in his own abilities. The young man is essentially a weak person who, when he is not thinking about his weakness, is contriving some magical solution to his problem as in the preceding dream.

He blames his father for his feelings of inferiority because the father has not set a good example for him. In one dream, for instance, all the tires on his car go flat for which he blames his father. "I am a flat tire just like my father." In another dream, he shows that this conception of his father is one of long standing.

I was at a race track observing the horses. I saw a little boy about three. His father was slouching alongside holding onto the rail all exhausted.

The little boy of three is the dreamer and the exhausted father is his own father.

The tragedy of this young man's life rests upon a self-conception of inadequacy taken over from his father, which prevents him from mastering his difficulties and which causes him to imagine highly improbable solutions for his inner conflicts.

In the normal course of development the feeling of hostility that the child has for the parent of the same sex is replaced by a sense of identification with that parent. The boy comes to regard his father and the girl her mother as a companion rather than as a rival. A strong feeling of camaraderie develops from the recognition on the part of the young person that "we are both men" or "we are both women." The boy tries to be like his father, the girl like her mother, so that bonds of common interests are forged. When this occurs the family triangle of love and hostility is weakened.

The next dream is a beautiful drama of a young man's identification with his father and brothers.

My dad and brothers and myself were traveling over a dangerous road winding around a mountain overlooking a valley, which had a wide river in it. We all felt excited and actually scared, although we thought we were daring and courageous, as we passed through dangerous passes in the road. Finally we reached the valley below, where we had to cross a small bridge. The bridge must have been small because we were walking over the bridge. As we approached the other side we noticed that there was a locked gate and no one was around to open it. It looked as though our trip was in vain. We all let out a discouraged or rather disappointed sound and started back on the way we came. Suddenly, however, a group of workmen nonchalantly opened up the gate and then started across the bridge apparently on their way to work over the path we had traveled. They shut the gate behind them but did not lock it so we all went through the gate to the other side.

They are traveling over a symbolic road of life, a road beset with dangers and frustrations, which they meet with manly courage and daring. The bridge symbolizes the transition from youth to maturity which at first is closed to the travelers but with the aid of other men becomes open. The workmen symbolize the dreamer's conception that one gets ahead in life by being industrious.

It often happens during the earlier stages of identification that the young person will turn against the former object of his love, the parent of the opposite sex, because he feels that the mother or father as the case may be is interfering with his efforts to achieve a good identification. A son may reject his mother and a daughter her father because the parent belongs to an out-group with alien interests and aspirations. This theme is strikingly developed in the following dream.

My mother was told by my aunt with whom I stay that I had wasted my money buying a book on human anatomy. My mother was very angry, stating how bad it was and how the pictures inside were dirty because they showed naked people. As she was protesting, my father and brothers came to my rescue, stating it was the best thing I ever did. My father said he was proud of me and it showed I was really going to become a great man. The dream ended with my father and brothers siding with me and my mother left stranded to her own thoughts of the uncleanliness of an anatomy book.

The mother is assigned the role of an antagonist who protests the dreamer's interest in sex while the father and brothers are protagonists, who take the dreamer's side and encourage him to be a man like themselves. The dreamer rejects the mother's way of life and adopts the values of men.

The weakening of the family triangle by identifying with the same sex parent does not entirely destroy the earlier conceptual patterns of a person. The prototypic view of the same sex parent as a dangerous rival for the love of the opposite sex parent persists in spite of later developments, and influences the person's conception of men and women throughout his life. No matter how much a man may feel at home with other men, they are still potential enemies. The same thing is true for women except that they, as already noted, are more likely to feel that both men and women are unfriendly.

The residual conceptions which have their origin in the family constellation help us to understand why the triangle theme in story and play has such a fascination for people. They see their own conflicts acted out before their very eyes. We understand, if but dimly, why Hamlet cannot revenge his father's murder. The reason is that the uncle has done what Hamlet has wanted from early childhood to do, namely murder his father and possess his mother. Was it not Diderot who said that the desire of every boy is to kill his father and sleep with his mother?

Greek mythology is filled with the theme of a son trying to take the place of his father, but in no play is it made more explicit than it is in *Oedipus Rex* by Sophocles. It has been predicted by the oracles that Oedipus would grow up to murder his father and marry his mother. This is precisely what happens despite the parents' efforts to thwart the fulfillment of the prophecy by abandoning Oedipus to the beasts of the forest. He miraculously escapes death and is adopted by the king and queen of a neighboring state. When Oedipus has grown to manhood he wages war on his own country, kills his father and takes his mother as a part of the victor's spoils. The stark portrayal of this theme is tempered by the fact that Oedipus does not know who his real parents are, nor do they know him, and when it does become known, Jocasta, his mother, commits suicide and Oedipus tears out his eyes in retribution.

By this time it must be apparent to those who are familiar with the writing of Freud that what he discovered in the early years of this century by treating emotionally disturbed patients we have verified by analyzing the dreams of normal people. Freud found in every one of his patients the existence of a repressed desire to do what Oedipus had done, or in the case of women, to murder the mother and marry the father. He called the system of ideas composing the family triangle the Oedipus complex and felt that it was a decisive factor in all mental disorders.

Our contribution has been one of demonstrating that the Oedipus complex as described by Freud is by no means limited to people who are mentally sick. It appears frequently as the source of anxiety in perfectly well people. For example, it explains why some men and some women are attracted solely to people who are already married or engaged. These people have a strong need to dispossess another person of his mate, a need which stems from the Oedipus complex. It also explains why some people never get married. A son feels that he must look after his mother and a daughter after her father. Of course they usually find good excuses to justify not getting married but below the surface one discerns the real reason, a strong attachment for the mother or father. In dreams we are permitted a view of the foundation upon which our relations with people are governed and the reasons why these relations generate so much anxiety.

7   Freedom Versus Security

THERE ARE two ways of life for man. One road leads him toward freedom and independence. It is the way of growth and maturity. The other road takes him back to security and dependence. It is the way of regression and immaturity. Man is forever making choices between these two roads. He travels a little way in one direction until he meets a roadblock then turns and goes for a while down the other way of life. Some men go farther in one direction than in the other, but whichever direction he goes his journey is attended by anxiety. If he aspires to be free and independent he encounters the specters of insecurity and aloneness. If he chooses to be secure and dependent he feels hemmed in and cowardly.

The basic reason for this conflict is found in the long childhood of the human species, a childhood during which the

individual becomes habituated to safety and comfort. His bodily
needs are satisfied and he is protected from physical dangers.
When he is hurt, his mother comforts him. When he is lost, he
is looked for until found. When he has a bad dream, he is taken
in bed with his parents. Although he experiences distress, there
is always someone to turn to for relief from his discomfort. He
learns to do things for himself and to accept responsibility
within the security of the family circle and the custody of the
school. During this period of life limitations on freedom are
compensated for by the rewards of safety.

As he grows older the restrictions become more onerous and
the rewards less satisfying. He wants to stand on his own feet
and make his own decisions, but when he tries to liberate himself
from the stifling oppression of dependence he encounters frustrations and hazards for which he has not been suitably pre-
pared. Isolated from the protective family circle he feels alone
and inadequate, so he runs back to the sanctuary of home.
During adolescence these leavings and returnings become more
frequent and they are attended by an increasing load of anxiety.

The strange antics of youth are largely explained by this
conflict between liberty and safety. At the same time that he is
rebelling against the restraints of family authority he is making
numerous demands upon his parents for money, clothes, food
and love. He accuses his family of trying to smother his in-
dividuality, yet he willingly sacrifices his precious autonomy to
the enslaving conventions of his peers. When he is given more
freedom and responsibility he condemns his parents for neglecting him. He mistakes license for liberty and by acting recklessly
and impulsively becomes more of a burden upon society. He

expects consideration from others yet gives little in return. These are some of the symptoms of the conflict between maturity and immaturity.

Although this conflict reaches its zenith in the late teens it is likely to recur whenever a person feels that he is unable to cope with the problems of life. A married woman returns to her parents after quarreling with her husband, or a man gets drunk when he loses his job. In times of personal danger, one turns to God or to the State, or to whatever gives promise of protection and comfort. At such times he sacrifices freedom for security.

This major conflict of man pervades his nocturnal thoughts. It is especially prominent in the dreams of young people, when the conflict is strongest, but it is also found in the dreams of older people. Young women seem to experience more anxiety in connection with this conflict than young men do. Whether this is due to some condition inherent in women or whether it is the result of special cultural influences, we cannot say. Nature and culture probably interact with each other in this case as they do to produce other differences between men and women.

The conflict appears in many forms and guises in dreams and the types of solutions offered are many and varied. Here, for example, is a dream reported by a young, unmarried woman.

I dreamed I was on a pier where a ship was about to leave. Standing next to me was my husband (not really, but a fellow I know). I was wearing two white orchids. I felt on the verge of tears. My mother was weeping bitterly. My dad and brother were sad too, but they didn't carry on so. The whistle blew. I knew it was our last chance to board the ship. I couldn't make up my mind. I looked at my mother and then at my husband, trying to decide.

Finally I put my arms around my mother and kissed her good-by. Then I turned to my husband, who put his arm around me and we slowly walked up the gangplank. At first I tried to keep the tears back. Then I broke down and cried and cried.

This dream is a straightforward representation of her problem, to leave home or stay with her family. The family members on the pier echo the grief of the dreamer as she looks first at her childhood protectors and then at her new adult companion and mate. The dreamer finally decides to take the path of maturity although it is a hard decision for her to make.

In the case of young women the choice is often framed between husband and home, while with young men leaving home to get married is less usual. They want to leave home in order to have more freedom, not to settle down with a wife. The following dream supplied by a young man in his early twenties typifies the masculine solution.

I was standing in front of an old white house in the winter. It apparently was the house I live in now. It looked very beautiful and the windows were lighted and it looked warm and inviting inside. I was going away, evidently never to return and was feeling very sad about it. I remember thinking that it was too bad that all those happy days had slipped by so rapidly without my realizing it and I wished I had taken better advantage of them. I awoke still feeling quite sad.

Although he is sorry to leave his inviting and cozy home in which he has spent so many happy days, he seems to have made up his mind to step out in the world and make an independent life for himself.

A young woman does not necessarily see marriage as the sole

means of escape from her family. She may picture herself getting a job and living in some distant city as this dreamer does.

A group of girls and I were having lunch in a restaurant. We were having lots of fun discussing our plans for the future of living in New York, being independent and working. To my surprise they all wanted to do it and we planned to get a joint apartment. Then we noticed that it was raining and we couldn't leave.

In order to avoid being alone, her plans for independence include other girls with whom she would live. This is a common solution in life as well as in dreams. The dream ends on a pessimistic note. They cannot leave because it is raining. In other words, the dreamer is not so sure that she wants to separate from her family, and the rain is introduced to provide her with a convenient excuse for staying where she is. In reporting this dream the young lady showed that she was aware of its significance by making the following comment.

I would like to be independent. Even though I'm very attached to my family, they wish to keep me a little girl forever. Also, there is nervous tension in our house because of illness and I'd like to live somewhere else but also come home frequently. The rain probably symbolized that I unconsciously don't want to leave. My happiness at everyone wanting a joint apartment probably meant that I want a few girls to go and live with me, as I wouldn't want to, nor would I be allowed to venture it alone.

The mistake she makes is to blame her parents for keeping her a little girl. Granted that she may have been babied; nevertheless it is her inner apprehension about being independent and facing adult responsibilities that is at fault. Notice, for instance, how she would like to put her relationship with her family on a commuter basis, leaving and returning home at rather frequent intervals.

This conception of a life line between the young person and her family is portrayed in an interesting symbolic way in the next dream.

I was riding along in a very large car with my parents and my younger brother and although I had no place to go I kept telling my father to drive faster. Nevertheless I was still very unhappy. My father could not seem to drive fast enough to please me. Finally I got very angry and told my parents that if they could drive no faster than that I would get out of the car and go by myself. I jumped out of the car while it was going at top speed. As I put my foot down on the road I floated upward instead of touching the ground. My clothes had changed completely. I was all dressed in a long white flowing dress and white sandals. I also had small silver wings but I did not use them. I floated through the air and then I would leap from one telephone pole to another, and rest on each one. I kept the car in sight so that I could come back and land on it when I wanted to. I did this from time to time and then I woke up.

Faster, faster, faster is the plea of the dreamer, but the family does not satisfy her urge for speed so she breaks away and assumes the form of a free-moving angel. However, she keeps home base in sight so she can return to it when she wants to. The silver cord is stretched but it is not broken.

The mixed feelings which a young person has about leaving home may be represented by the turmoil and confusion involved in getting to a train on time. This is the theme of the next dream in which a young woman is trying to catch a train to return to college.

I was in a car with someone on my way to a train. He or she let me off at an intersection just before a bridge under which my train was to stop. There were many people and many cars at the inter-section, and I was trying to be polite and let others go before me. I was so anxious for fear of missing my train, but I kept standing back for others. Finally I decided that I had to plow through and I did, getting to the opposite corner directly above the train stop. I heard the train coming and I rushed as fast as I could but I missed it. I was especially upset as that was the last train I could get in order to return to college for the Christmas activities. I wanted to cry, but I just couldn't seem to do so.

She wants to cry but does not because she knows that her failure to catch the train was intentional. Her politeness in letting other people go ahead of her is merely an excuse for finally missing the train. Observe also that it is the last train she can take so that having missed it she will have to stay home, which is her dominant wish. Had the pressure of her desire to leave her family been stronger than her urge to remain at home she would have caught the train. The bridge in this dream symbolizes as it does in so many dreams the transition between two periods in one's life.

Wedding dreams are a good deal more frequent among young women than among young men, and often in these dreams something happens to delay or stop the ceremony. In one such dream the ceremony was being performed in the midst of an air raid and people kept distracting the proceedings by running in and out of the church. In several wedding dreams the altar receded into the distance as the dreamer was walking down the aisle so that she never did reach it. One dreamer was at a wedding and everything was going according to plan except that the bride-groom did not appear. In another,

I dreamed that Fred, my boy friend, came home and we were to be married, but then we went into our living room and sat by the fire and seemingly forgot all about it.

As a rule when a young woman dreams about her own wedding, the bridegroom is either a stranger or someone for whom she has little affection. Rarely is it a close friend or fiancé. The appearance of the unexpected or strange man usually halts the wedding. Such an outcome reveals that the dreamer cannot really conceive of herself getting married and leaving home. She is afraid of trying something new and strange. In contrast to the wedding dreams of women, when young men dream of marriage their weddings proceed without interruption and their brides are girls whom they expect and want to marry. Apparently they do not experience the same apprehension about marriage that women do. Marriage does not symbolize the breaking of family ties for men as it does for women.

Conceptions of what it means to separate from the family are numerous. One dreamer sees it as walking alone on a vast empty desert. Another pictures it as being exposed to unfriendly elements.

I was out in a large field with no trees or houses in sight, and I was all alone. Suddenly it all got dark and a wind came up and it began to rain very hard. I remember I was in my pajamas and I was very cold. I began running but I couldn't move. Finally I was so tired that I lay down and went to sleep.

A young man visualizes his conception of being lost by not being able to find the right road. "Wrong road" implies that the way of life he has chosen is morally wrong.

I was driving a car on a single lane in the country, and as I passed into the valley I realized I was on the wrong road. Then the dream changed to a view of two roads branching off in the form of a triangle, and again I felt lost.

Another young man uses the metaphor of a boat drifting aimlessly at sea.

I dreamed I was afloat in a rowboat, drifting without oars and wondering helplessly whether or not I would drift ashore or out to sea. I awoke still drifting helplessly with the tide and nowhere near land.

The land represents security and the open sea stands for the hazards of independence. The fact that he is without oars implies that he is not equipped to guide his life but must leave it to fate, symbolized by the tide, to take him where it will. In other words he lacks the necessary competence and confidence to solve this problem through his own efforts. This same person had the following dream.

I was alone in my hotel room waiting to ship out. I was sick and in bed and lonely. I was so lonely that I decided to "buy" a woman to keep me happy until my ship sailed.

The thought of shipping out to sea makes him feel lonely and he decides to buy some companionship to efface the thought of leaving the safety of land. Going to sea or running away to sea has always signified a more or less complete break with one's home and family. Robinson Crusoe is an example of this basic metaphor and its appeal to young people arises from the fact that Crusoe does succeed in making a go of things without any help from anyone when he is shipwrecked on an uninhabited island.

Separation anxiety may also express itself in the form of

threats and dangers which the dreamer encounters when he
is away from home. The usual result of a frightening experience
is to evoke in the dreamer a wish to return to the protection
of the family. This state of affairs is illustrated in the following dream.

I was in a house with a lot of girls. It was on a main street
where streetcars ran. Across the street were four men and one of
them knocked another one down and shot him. The men ran toward
the house where we were and we were scared to death. Two police
were there protecting us from the bandits, who had run around
the house somewhere. The policemen had their pistols all ready
to shoot if one of the bandits should appear. There was a streetcar
waiting to leave right beside our house, but it wasn't going near
my home. A friend of one of the girls picked her up, and I begged
the girl to take me home, but she wasn't going my way either. I
kept trying to call my dad to ask him to come after me. The policemen left and there were only two of us girls left in the house. We
were afraid to go out on the street and wait for a streetcar for fear
the men would return. There was a drunk under a back window
of the house and we hung out the window and tried to keep him
quiet so he wouldn't attract the bandit's attention to the house.

When the dreamer finds herself in danger, her first thought is
to get back home. When this does not work out, she tries
to call her father to come and get her but this too is unsuccessful. Even the policemen, who prove to be inadequate protectors, desert her, and she is left alone in the house with two
other girls. The drunk outside represents the dreamer's conception of uncontrolled impulses which are likely to get her in
more trouble if they attract the attention of the bandits. This
dream mirrors the terrible consequences that result from letting

one's impulses go and how desirable it would be under such circumstances to return to the safety and moral restraints of the family.

Another dream in which the dreamer conceives of home as a place of refuge from the dangers of the outside world is this one.

I dreamed I was with a crowd of schoolgirls getting on a bus. Just then a very tall man came up in back of me and tried to pick me up. I got on the bus just in time before he could catch me although I don't remember him chasing me. All at once we were driving down the street in front of my house and I felt if I could just get off here at my house I would be safe.

The thought of being attacked by a man, which is really a seduction wish on the part of the dreamer, scares her so much that she wants to return home.

In some dreams the conflict between freedom and security is resolved by the dreamer taking a trip with her parents. In this way she can enjoy a certain measure of freedom and new experiences without sacrificing the protection offered by the family. Yet even this solution is not always satisfactory. One young woman dreamed she was traveling in Japan with her parents but she did not like the trip because everything was so different. Consequently she got on a bus which would take her back to her home town. In commenting upon this dream, the dreamer said that she does not like to travel even with her parents because she feels strange in new places and longs to get back to the daily routine of home life. Safety for her lies not so much in the family circle as it does in the security of familiar surroundings and the protection of a settled way of life.

The same theme is present in the next dream.

"I always wanted to move to the country," I told Mother and Dad, but they told me that we had to wait to build. It seemed far off and, thinking I would probably be married before that happened, I was disappointed. Then somehow I found out that our house had been sold and that this was the last night I would be in our house. A feeling of nostalgia crept over me as I looked about my room. There I had grown up, been sick, dressed for my first date, had many confidential talks, had dressed for my sister's wedding, had the surprise of having it redecorated while away at my first year of college, etc., etc., and suddenly I decided that I couldn't leave. "Why, oh, why was the house sold?" I bemoaned. I made up my mind to watch them move out the furniture and then go to my room, lock the door and just stay there. I was sure that no one would notice my not leaving, too.

It is the security of place and not the security of family that is uppermost in this girl's mind. In the language of bull fighting, her old home is her *querencia,* a place in the ring where the bull feels safe and from which it is well-nigh impossible for the matador to dislodge him once he has taken it into his head to remain there.

In some dreams the dreamer pictures herself trying desperately to return home. Such a dream is this one.

I was trying to buy a train ticket for home. People kept getting in my way and keeping me from the ticket window. I had only a few minutes to catch the train. When I finally did get the ticket I couldn't find the train. I kept getting on the wrong tracks and going on the wrong trains. At last I found the right ramp and got on the train. I found my sister's boy friend on the train and kissed him. There was only one thing wrong, the train was going the wrong way.

Her mixed feelings about returning home are symbolized by the obstacles which interfere with her finding the right train. The repeated use of the word "wrong" refers to the moral wrongness she feels because she kisses her sister's boy friend. By this improper act she cuts herself off even more from her home.

Another dream of the same general type but with a different ending is this one reported by a young woman.

I was sitting on an old rusty boxcar with several other young people. It was in the desert. Next I was buying a train ticket to go home. I was afraid I wouldn't get a ticket but I did without any trouble.

Having succeeded in getting away from her family she discovers that being free from parental restrictions does not give her the satisfaction she expected. Her fear of not being able to get a ticket symbolizes her concern about being accepted by the family whom she has renounced.

One aspect of the freedom-versus-security conflict is the person's desire for a larger life space than that provided by his home. He feels confined by the short radius of the family circle and wants to break through the outer boundary into a larger world. This conception of a more spacious life is represented in one dream series by large, impressive, modern houses. The choice of mansions in this series is a compromise between two opposing forces, the need for more freedom and the contrary need for the security of home. By enlarging her home she obtains more liberty without sacrificing the protection which a home provides. This is a typical dream from her series.

I was in a very large house, one that I had never been in before. Each room that I went in was different than the one before. The furnishings were in modern style and the colors were bright. I was amazed at the beauty of the home and the elegance of the furnishings.

This dream conveys in addition to the idea of largeness conceptions of modernity and elegance. She wants a newer, richer life as well as a more expanded one.

The contrast between what she has and what she wants is depicted in another dream.

I was standing before an easel, painting a scene. It was of two houses, one very pretty and modern and the other very old and rather nondescript. Suddenly I decided I wanted to visit the new house, so I did. There were people in it but none of them was familiar to me. I remember looking out over some water.

Her present life is old and nondescript, the one she desires is pretty and modern. Even the people in the house she visits are new to her. That her present life bores her is brought out in this dream.

People were going through our house, as though they were looking it over to buy it. For a while I danced, but soon I became bored so I went outside and decided to take a walk.

She would like to get away from the monotony of her present life, but not too far away from the protection afforded by her family, as the next dream shows.

I was evidently taking a short ride in the car for the purpose of hunting for a house. The one particular street I remember going up was the street next to the one I live on. Soon I stopped the car and got out to look at the inside of a house. It seemed to be very large and I kept walking and walking. Then I woke up.

By finding a large house which is located close by her present home, she effects a compromise between her conflicting needs. The endless walking symbolizing her relentless but fruitless search for a life of greater freedom.

Her frustration is more clearly portrayed in the next dream.

I was walking down a very nice street in Chicago. The houses on it were attractive and there was an air of middle-class substantialness about them. I noticed the pretty lawns and trees lining the walk. As I was in the market for a house I decided to buy one of them. But suddenly I noticed railroad tracks to my left and the atmosphere seemed to change. I looked over to where the houses had been and everything seemed to recede in the distance. There were hills and little buildings and winding paths.

Just as she is about to purchase an attractive, substantial house in a distant city, the setting recedes into the distance. Her goal is not so easy to reach as she has thought. The transition in this dream represents as it always does a change in the dreamer's conception. Having visualized herself buying a house in another city, she then notices the railroad tracks which symbolize leaving home and realizes how impossible it is for her to leave her family at the present time. The receding scene places the fulfillment of her wish well into the future.

In one of her dreams the young woman returns to a house in which she lived when she was a child. This regression is interesting because it fits in with her current wish for a larger life space. To a child one's home always seems much larger than it does to an adult. The physical house does not change in size but the person's conception of it does, partly because he is physically larger and partly because his requirements for greater freedom of action have increased. By returning to a childhood home which seems in memory to have been a very large one she satisfies her desire for more room. Were she actually to revisit her old home, our dreamer would find, as so many others have, that the mansion she expects to see is only a house of ordinary size.

In several other dreams she is in a beautiful castle, a mansion or a large house. In one dream she is steering a large cabin cruiser on a big lake. In another she is walking along the beach and sees a sand castle which has been built by a small boy. "I stopped, fascinated by the castle." Her craving for space is so intense that she sees impressive dwellings wherever she goes, even sand castles on the beach.

We conclude this chapter with a dream series in which the conflict between the desire to live an independent life and the need for security provided by the family pervades practically all of the dreams. The dreamer, a young woman twenty years old, displays considerable ingenuity in her search for a satisfying solution.

The nature of the conflict is clearly set forth in the following spotlight dream.

I dreamed that I volunteered to go overseas as a teacher. I went to Italy to teach the children there. My dream consisted of leaving my family and being graciously welcomed in Italy by an Army officer and his wife. I was married shortly after my arrival there. Most of my dream was about the difficulty I had leaving home.

In this dream she manages to get away from home, yet, in spite of the presence of parent substitutes in Italy, the Army officer and his wife, and a speedy marriage, most of the dream is concerned with her difficulty in leaving home. That the dreamer is aware of her conflict is indicated by the explanatory comment appended to the dream report.

I guess this dream has to do with my fear of leaving home. I have never been away for more than a week and my folks keep insisting it would be wise for me to leave for a while.

In the next dream she tries to satisfy her parents by taking a trip but even though she has the companionship of her sister she cannot find the right train.

I dreamed last night I was in a train station with my sister. We were supposed to make a certain train, but for some reason neither of us could find the right track. It was most confusing and all I can remember is the two of us racing about trying to find that train in a large depot that had many tracks and entrances.

The next dream, a regressive one, serves the purpose of enabling her to avoid the necessity of making a choice between family security and personal freedom.

I dreamed I was back in high school again.

If she were younger, neither her own need for independence nor the pressure from her parents to act grown-up would be so insistent. However this solution does not satisfy her so she modifies the regression in the following manner.

My dream last night was quite confusing. I was attending college classes but was in high school. I was in the high-school building attending classes with my high-school friends, but the classes themselves were those I now attend. It was rather a review of a typical day as I used to have them in high school. We were planning to attend a football game after school and things were quite exciting.

Intellectually she wants to be in college; emotionally she would be happier if she were still in high school. Thus she resorts to the compromise of attending college classes in her old high-school building, as though to say, "Intellectually I am an adult, emotionally and socially I am still an adolescent."

Another solution, although a bitter one, is presented in the next dream.

I dreamed I got infantile paralysis and found I would have a permanent affliction. I had to quit school and life seemed pretty miserable.

She is even willing to endure infantile paralysis or become a paralyzed infant in order to resolve the conflict. Obviously she would have to remain home and be taken care of by her family if she did contract infantile paralysis. The next dream is of the same type but involves a less serious disorder.

I dreamed I had an accident and broke my leg. The rest of the dream I was in the hospital getting just loads of attention and sympathy. Friends came to see me and one of my overseas friends was even given a furlough to come home for a while. The pain I might have had from a broken leg never entered the dream. It was all very pleasant and I was the center of attention.

The fractured leg, like infantile paralysis, immobilizes her so that she cannot leave home. Furthermore she receives a lot of secondary gain in the form of attention and sympathy. These gratifications are however merely by-products of her primary wish to remain in the family circle.

The conflict between independence and security even affects her feelings about her boy friend. One dream expresses a wish that he would come back to her, another signifies that she wants him to leave her alone.

I dreamed again last night that a friend of mine who is a German prisoner was returned home.

I dreamed I went to church one Sunday and one of our members, who has been reported missing overseas, was there. Before he left we had been good friends—but for some reason he refused to even speak to me. I was quite put out and couldn't understand the reason for his actions.

The relation of these two dreams to her basic conflict is fairly obvious. On the one hand she wants a husband, on the other hand marriage means leaving her family, an idea which she is not ready to accept. If he would reject her, as he does in the second dream, she could postpone a decision.

Her resourcefulness in trying to solve her conflict is seen in the following dream.

I dreamed that my family and I took a trip out west.

She manages to get away from home by taking her family with her.

The dreamer is willing to go to almost any extremes to handle her problem, even to the extent of having her mother die.

I dreamed my mother was very ill and after much anguish died. It was pretty gruesome.

The death of her mother would be a good solution for several reasons. In the first place it would remove the source of pressure on the dreamer to grow up since that is what the mother is insisting she do. In the second place it would enable the girl to take over her mother's place in the family thereby making it unnecessary for her to leave home. Moreover, by substituting for her mother she would be playing the role of homemaker for her father, a position she very much covets. Finally, if that solution did not work out, the death of her mother would cause the dissolution of the family and the dreamer would be left with no other alternative except to shift for herself.

The anxiety generated by the idea of growing up is pictured in the next dream.

Last night I dreamed about the first day of this summer session. I couldn't seem to get to classes on time and the textbooks weren't available. I was terrifically upset and felt as if the situation was too involved for me to cope with. I woke up this morning worn out from that experience in which I was at a loss and felt very defeated.

Why does the beginning of a new term trouble her so? In the first place, it is the repetition of an earlier experience of separation, the first day she left home to go to school. Each time a new session begins, it echoes the anxiety she felt when she started in the first grade. Practically every child has had the same experience, but in our dreamer's case it has dogged her for fourteen years. In addition the first day of a new college session brings her that much closer to graduation and the consequent necessity for assuming responsibility for her own life. Many college students as they near graduation have similar misgivings; some of them employ such strategies as not finishing their work or failing in their studies or becoming ill in order to postpone the dreaded graduation day.

Granted that the conflict between progression and regression is fairly common, if not universal, among young people, why has it become so intense in this dreamer? Why does she feel so inadequate? Why must she always run away from maturity? The last dream of the series suggests an answer.

Last night I dreamed my sister and I were in a play. All I had to do was sing a song, but they didn't give it to me until the last minute and I couldn't seem to learn the song. My sister had the lead and for some reason I was always appearing on the stage when I wasn't supposed to. I did sing my song finally and it turned out to be a success, much to my surprise.

This dream is a classical example of the rivalry between sisters. Her sister has the "lead" and the dreamer intrudes when she is not wanted. In other words the dreamer feels that her parents have rejected her and favored her sister. Her craving for security is very strong because she has experienced so much insecurity. Furthermore as she has already told us, her parents are beginning to insist that she get away from home and this parental pressure is interpreted by the dreamer as another sign of rejection. The final dream ends reassuringly. She sings her song successfully. Whether her transition to full maturity will be as easy is problematical. Since she has felt rejected throughout her life it is questionable whether the "singing of her song" will be as simple as it is in the dream. Even the dreamer has some reservations about the outcome since the song turned out to be a success "much to my surprise." Her battle for maturity is by no means won.

In this chapter we have taken account of the besetting problem of the young person who stands at the threshold of maturity. Should he step over that threshold into a world of adult responsibility and lonely independence or should he stay his foot and remain within the snug harbor of the family circle? Argument and counter-argument weave themselves through his dreams. The step is made, and the next moment, regretting the impulsive deed, he rushes back into the house and slams the door against maturity. Sometimes when he wishes to return he finds the door closed against him and so he sits and weeps like a lost child. On other occasions, he learns, to his dismay, that many dangers lurk in the world outside and that his fortitude is insufficient. Tormented by fears of the unknown and goaded by the relentless forces of growth, he wavers at one of the crucial choice points of his life. Should he go forward to maturity or should he retrace his steps to immaturity? This is the conflict of youth.

8   The Moral Conflict

THE PROBLEM of right and wrong has always plagued man and he has devoted not a little time and energy throughout history to the formulation of standards of conduct by which he might distinguish good from evil. Yet it is not so much a question of learning the difference between right and wrong as it is one of his avoiding clearly recognized temptations. The moral code of Christianity as set forth in the Ten Commandments is stated in such simple, comprehensible language that surely everyone who hears them must understand what he is supposed to do in order to live virtuously. Why then does man continue to dishonor his parents, covet his neighbor's possessions, lie, steal, kill and commit adultery when he knows better?

The answer it seems to me is obvious. Man finds it impossible to live a completely virtuous life because his impulses, especially those of sex and aggression, often become stronger than the prohibitions against these impulses. When this takes place man sins, and he sins with full awareness of what he is doing. Pressure from within and temptation from without conspire to make him break his moral code.

The usual consequence of violating a moral precept is for the sinner to feel guilty. He suffers remorse and vows to do better in the future. For a while he may hold to his resolution, until the impulse and temptation become too great; then again he transgresses the code and again he feels ashamed. Like the cycle of night and day, man swings back and forth between the poles of good and evil.

Why does man feel guilty when he does something bad? Primarily because he has a conscience which has the power to punish him. This kind of anxiety is called moral anxiety or feelings of guilt. Where does the conscience come from and why does it have the power to punish the person by making him feel anxious? Conscience is the internalized voice of society as spoken by the parents. The child learns the difference between right and wrong from his parents. Moreover, he finds out that when he is good he is rewarded by approval and presents and when he is bad he is punished by harsh words and spankings. Consequently, when his conscience develops, it not only represents the sanctions and prohibitions of his parents as agents of society but it also contains the power to reward and punish. The rewards of conscience are feelings of virtue while the punishments are feelings of guilt.

Unfortunately for man he cannot avoid feeling sinful by merely behaving in accordance with the dictates of conscience.

A wicked thought is as bad as a wicked deed. In fact a man who is tempted but does not yield may feel even more guilty than one who does. The evil doer can usually find excuses by which to justify his behavior while the evil thinker cannot so easily rationalize his desire to do something bad. Which is to say the moral conflict is probably stronger for saints than it is for sinners.

We are all sinners in our dreams. When we are asleep and are deprived of the external controls of waking life our mind turns to thoughts of impulse gratification. It has already been pointed out in an earlier chapter that sexual and aggressive themes are very common in dreams. We often do things in our dreams that we would not dream of doing in waking life. Obviously these dream misdeeds are only imaginary; they exist only as thoughts in our mind. Yet the mere fact of having a bad thought causes us, in our dreams, to feel guilty, and what started out as a gratifying wish-fulfillment dream ends by being a nightmare.

The conflict between impulse and conscience is nowhere seen to better advantage than it is in dreams. For it is in dreams that the mind gives full play to the coarser motives, with a resulting surge of condemnation from the conscience. Although the dreamer has greater freedom to think about the gratification of wishes, he is at the same time placed in the position of experiencing more anxiety than he ordinarily feels in waking life. Crime and punishment function as cause and effect in the internal state of dreams to a far greater extent than they do in the external state of waking life.

Let us look at the following dream.

I killed a tramp and then a hotel porter, whom I beat over the head, because he found out about my crime. The first thing I remember clearly is that I was at the inquest. The room was very similar to that of a hospital ward, and all the people concerned in the proceedings were lying in the beds as was I. Present were my father, my mother, my twenty-one-year-old brother and my thirteen-year-old brother. There were several witnesses called and they all testified that I had undoubtedly committed the crimes. I was the last one to be called. When I was questioned, the person examining me did not ask direct questions, but rather seemed to steer away from any questions that might implicate me. I was aware that I had shrewdly passed his questions and he had not gotten anything from me. When he finished his questions, I went back and lay on my bed. As I lay thinking, I knew that I was guilty and wondered why they had not asked me if I had committed the murders. Unable to stand the anxiety any longer, I jumped up from the bed and told them to question me further and to be sure and ask me if I had committed the crimes. They asked me and I confessed. I went back to the bed and lay down. I started thinking of my girl and what effect this would all have on her. I became frightened and hoped she'd never learn it because then I'd be sure she would never marry me. I then became aware of the disapproving look of my parents. Then I awoke in a cold sweat.

The young man has committed two murders and then finds himself in a hospital ward where an investigation is being held. This type of setting suggests that the dreamer conceives of himself as being sick; in fact, his whole family is sick since they occupy beds also. He is saying in effect that crime is a kind of sickness for which the person is not responsible. However, this explanation does not satisfy the dreamer, so an investigation is held during which he matches his wits successfully against an incompetent examiner who symbolizes his conscience. Instead of walking out a free man, however, the dreamer is overwhelmed by moral anxiety until it becomes unbearable and he has to confess. This act of confession should and does relieve his guilt but it also produces a new type of fear: what will his girl and his parents think of him? By submitting to the voice of conscience which makes him confess he has become involved with real dangers from his environment. Reality anxiety or fear of something in the external world takes the place of moral anxiety or fear of conscience. This is one of the painful dilemmas which faces a person suffering from a guilty conscience. He can try to endure his inner feelings of shame and remorse or he can confess and run the risk of being punished by society. In either case there is no crime without punishment.

The policeman is a favorite personification of conscience in dreams because he represents law and order and because he arrests people for misconduct. The following dream of a young man is a typical policeman dream.

I was talking with a companion, and had a revolver in my hand. He had handed it to me, and was laughing at me, for an officer of the law was approaching, and I was to be impounded for carrying a dangerous weapon.

The dreamer is to be punished for carrying a dangerous weapon. Since gun not only stands for an aggressive instrument but also symbolizes a conception of masculine sexuality, the dreamer feels guilty over the manifestation of the two impulses, sex and aggression.

There are many dreams in which the dreamer is arrested for speeding, for going through a red light, or for other traffic violations. As we have already pointed out, automobile stands for sexual impulsivity, so it follows that a traffic violation signifies the dreamer's conception of sexual misconduct, for which he is then punished by being arrested.

Sometimes the policeman appears in dreams as a protector and not as a punisher. In such cases the dreamer is appealing to his conscience to prevent him from committing a lawless act. For example a male dreamer got mixed up with a gang of thugs and finally called the police to come and arrest them. This served the purpose of arresting the expression of his own wicked impulses. A young woman had the following dream.

I dreamed that at Christmas time four girls including myself were staying at my home. It was broadcast over the radio that a convict was at large. He came in our front door where the Christmas tree was placed and chased us. We finally got him out the back door and called the police.

The convict represents the dreamer's conception of her own impulses and she calls the police to protect her against their lawlessness.

One dreamer committed a crime while masquerading as a policeman, a strategy by which he tries to give official sanction to the gratification of an impulse in order to avoid punishment. The strategy does not work, however, for his masquerade is seen through by real policemen who chase him.

A slightly different version of the policeman-as-conscience dream is the following one in which a fireman appears.

I was standing on my neighbor's front porch, when a fire inspection car pulled up to the curb. An officer got out, looked at me, and told me that I was to come with him to be put in the police line-up as a suspected character in a false fire alarm report that was turned in the preceding night from an adjacent corner. It seemed they were bringing in all of the young men in the neighborhood. I protested that I had to go to school the next day and some other details, but to no avail. He still insisted that I come along.

The dreamer along with the other young men of the neighborhood is suspected of having turned in a false fire alarm. Fire is an objective representation of sexual passion and its association with false alarm in this dream suggests that the dreamer is anxious over masturbation or homosexuality, which are false or unnatural kinds of sexual expression.

Conscience in dreams may also be personified by Army officers, teachers, supervisors, judges, wardens, ministers and other people who exercise authority.

A common emblem for a repressive conscience is automobile brakes as exemplified in the following dream of a man.

I was in my automobile driving along and I wanted to stop the car immediately, but my brakes would not work. This went on and on until I awakened. I remember very vividly stepping on the brake, knowing that I must stop the car to avoid some danger, but the car would not stop. Horror-stricken and afraid, I kept applying my foot to the brake but nothing seemed to happen. There seemed to be a force or drive that made me keep moving in spite of the fact that I realized that I must stop and that this could be accomplished only by application of the brake.

The dreamer tells us that he had been making love to a girl the night before he had this dream and during their more passionate moments he kept reminding himself, "I have to put on the brakes before we go too far." He had succeeded in controlling himself in the actual waking life situation but his dream tells another story.

A curb, rail or fence can stand for the restraint of conscience. In one dream a young man and his girl were sitting on a curb, in another the dreamer and his girl were kissing over a fence, and in a third the dreamer was standing with her boy friend at the rail of a ship watching the huge waves. In this last dream the waves symbolize the dreamer's conception of the surge of lustful feeling which fills her mind, yet a railing prevents her from being submerged by passion.

That cleanliness is next to godliness is a sentiment which enjoys considerable popularity in western civilization, especially in the United States, where the bathtub or shower is looked upon as a necessity of life. By the same token dirt and the devil are boon companions. One can have a dirty body or a dirty mind. A dirty mind is one which thinks about sex, for sex is considered by many to be wicked. Soap and water are the enemies of moral as well as physical dirtiness. A mother washes out her child's mouth with soap for saying a dirty word and one is purified of his sins by baptism. It is not surprising, therefore, that taking a bath should be used in dreams to convey the idea of moral purification. This is portrayed in the following dream of a young man.

I dreamed I was taking a hot bath. The tub was almost filled and I was deeply submerged. All about me stood men and women, none of whom did I know. They pointed at me and made gestures of disgust and I tried to sink beneath the water to hide myself. They seemed to think I was dirty and that I did not often take a bath, and these things they said in their remarks. Suddenly they all seemed to walk out and I was alone and the water disappeared. I got out of the tub and looked at myself all over and saw that I was clean, and I cursed them.

The dreamer's guilt feelings are represented objectively by the people who accuse him of being dirty. This is an example of projecting one's inner feelings onto the outside world. By immersing himself in the hot bath he washes away his moral anxiety. Now that he is clean he turns aggressively on his accusers whose accusations are no longer justified. In effect what he is doing is cursing his own harsh conscience to which nevertheless he submits.

Although conscience develops by the internalization of prohibitions erected and enforced by parental authority, the process is not necessarily reversible. Impulses that were condemned in childhood by parents may be condoned by them or by society when the child grows up but this does not mean that the conscience automatically becomes more lenient as external restraints are relaxed. It happens more frequently than one might think that sexual relations between husband and wife are not enjoyed because the husband's or wife's conscience retains its old conception that sex is dirty. Sexually frigid men and women are the products of a society which forces the child and adolescent to think that sex is something base and wicked.

This irreversibility of conscience is depicted in the following dream of a young man.

I was in the bedroom of my house with a girl I know fairly well. It seems that, although I would like to have had sexual relations with her, I had already made up my mind that I would be clean and prohibit myself from any actions of my sexual desires with her. As we stood talking in the room, my mother came in but seemed unperturbed at finding us in the bedroom as she normally probably would have been. Nevertheless, I felt guilty and kept trying to think of ways to show her that I was clean and not guilty even though she wasn't in the least suspicious of me. Then she showed great affection for the girl by hugging her. Next I was met by my father in a similar situation with the same results. I felt guilty although he wasn't in the least suspicious of anything and though the girl and I were just having a friendly conversation. The reason I could tell they weren't in the least suspicious was that they acted so friendly and naturally as in any other situation. The girl seemed to be lifeless in that she showed no emotion or feelings in the dream.

This dreamer continues to feel guilty about desiring to have sexual relations with his girl in spite of the fact that his parents behave as though they would not interfere with and might even sanction sexual gratification. They are brought into the dream to relieve the dreamer's guilt but it does not succeed because the dreamer's conscience is stronger than the imputed permissiveness of the parents. The cold and lifeless girl is another defense against sexual consummation. Notice also the reiteration of the word "clean" in connection with moral conduct.

In another dream, similar to the last one but dreamed by a young woman, she is in bed with a man when her mother walks in. It is all right, though, because they are covered with a white sheet. The dreamer is saying, "You see, mother, you have nothing to fear because we are pure." In the language of conceptions, the dreamer is really saying, "My conscience has nothing to fear because even if I did go to bed with a man I would remain pure."

One of the favorite devices by which the dreamer expresses the various facets of his personality is to have each facet personified by a different dream character. As we have already seen a policeman and a criminal represent conscience and impulse respectively. In the following dream, the strife between a good brother and a wicked brother symbolizes the dreamer's conception of his moral conflict.

I dreamed that I was watching a movie or standing in the dark watching two men who were brothers. They were almost the same age or else they were twins. One was good and the other was bad. The bad brother kept trying to kill the good brother. The good brother was a little wiser and stronger than the bad brother; and each time the bad brother tried to kill him, the good brother would foil the attempt and save himself without hurting the bad brother and without attempting to retaliate. At last the bad brother tried to drown the good brother, but again he did not succeed.

This dream cannot be motivated by rivalry between brothers because the dreamer has no brothers. The fact that the dream characters are of the same age and that they are closely related to each other suggests that the brothers are projections of the dreamer's Jekyll and Hyde character. The inability of the wicked brother to overcome the virtuous one shows that the dreamer conceives of his good side as being stronger than his bad side. Moreover, his conscience is not thought of as being cruel and vindictive as it so often is in dreams. It controls his base nature by its superior intelligence rather than by punishment and hostility. This conception of conscience is rare indeed and indicates that it has been wholesomely integrated with the total personality.

Speaking of the punishing conscience one finds in dreams

wide latitude in the severity of punishment visited upon the dreamer. He may get off with a mild rebuke or a token punishment such as being given a traffic ticket or having to stay in after school. The other extreme is portrayed in the following dream.

I dreamed I was sentenced to death by a civil court. I walked down death row very calmly but protesting the execution as I was innocent. They strapped me into the electric chair, and pulled the switch. I awoke in a cold sweat.

If the punishment fits the crime then this young dreamer must have done something pretty bad to merit capital punishment. Protesting his innocence is an ineffectual defense because if he had been innocent he would not have had the dream.

Another way in which a person may attempt to subdue his moral anxiety in regard to sex is illustrated in the dream series of a young man. For him, as for Tannhäuser, there are two kinds of love, virtuous or sacred love and carnal or profane love. Then he divides women into two classes, those that are pure and respectable, like Tannhäuser's sainted Elizabeth, who are to be loved tenderly, and those that are promiscuous and seductive, like Tannhäuser's Venus, who are to be loved carnally. One marries a good girl and seduces or is seduced by a bad one. Sexual relations with loose women arouse little or no moral anxiety since "that is what they are for."

Our dreamer goes with a girl whom he expects to marry and when she is in his dreams their love-making is tender and controlled, as in the following dream.

I was studying for a psychology test with my girl. We were lying on the bed in her room reviewing our notes and asking each other questions about them. Except as each topic would come up instead of discussing psychology I would demonstrate a different point in making love to her. But although each type of love-making seemed different it never got beyond the kissing stage.

The setting is appropriate for sexual relations but their sensuality never goes beyond the kissing stage. And it never does, whether in dreams or waking life, as long as his girl is present. Let another type of girl enter his dreams and the outcome is quite different as in this dream.

I was visiting at the house of a girl I had known about a year ago. She and I were sitting on the couch talking to her mother— who shortly left us. The girl then began making very sexual love to me. I was rather surprised, but thought, "What the heck, why let a good thing go by?" Then we were undressed and having intercourse.

Here conscience does not assert itself, since it is obvious to the dreamer that this girl is a prostitute type. In another dream, he makes his ideas about such women even plainer. He is having sexual relations but he is not conscious of any other part of his partner save her genital area. For him a woman who indulges in sexual relations is no woman at all. She is just a penetrable organ.

This young man's main problem is to effect an integration of the romantic kind of love demanded by his conscience with the profane type of love demanded by his sexuality. Of course, he may do as many men do—marry for love and keep a mistress or visit prostitutes for sex. Unfortunately wives do not always appreciate this solution.

The division of women into good and bad types is frequently made along class lines. Men from upper-middle-class homes will treat women of their own class with respect and seduce girls of a lower class whom they meet at dance halls, skating rinks, taverns or along the street. The choice of sexual partner matches their conception of sex as a lower and base desire. Women often have the same feelings about lower-class men or foreigners. D. H. Lawrence made such a woman his central character in *Lady Chatterley's Lover.*

We conclude this chapter with the dream series of a young man who uses a variety of symbols to represent the conflicting conceptions of impulse and conscience. In the first dream his wayward impulses are personified by a criminal and his conscience by policemen.

All I can remember of the dream is that a party of us seemed to be running away from something, at times, the police, although I don't remember actually seeing any. The man they were seeking seemed to be small, deformed and a notorious criminal. This was only an impression because like the police I don't actually remember seeing him. We were hiding in all sorts of places. I couldn't understand what I was doing with this character for whom I had a feeling of revulsion.

The cloak of invisibility cast over the police and the criminal shows that his mind is not quite able to transform ideas into images. They remain as impressions although they are thought of as people. The dreamer conceives of his impulses as deformed, notorious, revolting and lawless.

In the next dream a policeman overtakes the dreamer while he is speeding down a long sloping hill.

I was out driving in the country. I had the feeling that it was in New York. I was going down a long, sloping hill and the car speeded up a little bit. At the bottom of the hill I was overtaken by a speed cop. He was an old fellow with a white flowing beard. He looked something like one of the "Keystone Kops." Somehow I knew he was coming before he even got there. I tried to explain that the car I was driving couldn't even get above forty miles per hour. I think I might have convinced him.

The dreamer tries to allay his anxiety by turning the police officer into a comic figure and by insisting that his automobile could not go very fast. The speeding car, here as elsewhere in dreams, symbolizes uncontrolled impulsivity. The statement "I knew he was coming before he even got there" indicates that the dreamer was aware of feeling guilty before this conception became materialized in the form of a policeman. It is as though we were actually seeing an abstract idea become a concrete image. The dream ends on a note of doubt as to whether his conscience has actually been convinced that he has not been behaving improperly.

In the next dream, getting on a wrong train is the emblem of misconduct and putting on the brakes is the symbol of moral pressure.

I remember being at a train ticket window. I guess I was buying a ticket. The girl at the ticket window kissed me in a way that seemed to give promise of better things when I returned from wherever I was going. I got on the train and it looked like the inside of a boxcar. I knew I was on the wrong train and I believe I tried to get somebody to pull the cord of the air brake.

The wrong conduct is here identified as sexual in character since the ticket girl's kiss gives promise of better things. Before he

can get back to these "better things," however, his conscience
steps in to call a halt.

Moral wrongness is represented in the next dream by being
in the wrong class.

I was in a large classroom filled with students. As I sat there I
suddenly had the feeling that I was in the wrong class. I was very
miserable, or perhaps a better word would be embarrassed. Finally
either because the instructor looked the other way or was otherwise
occupied, I found an opportunity to slip out. In the next room
there were also many people. I found a seat about halfway to the
back of the room and suddenly realized that this was a church
service. Although I didn't recognize the speaker I knew he was a
minister and I liked him very much. In the back of the room, a
group of people, women, I think, were talking away and not paying attention to what was going on in the front of the room.

He slips out of the wrong class in which he feels embarrassed
and goes into another classroom in which a church service is
being held. The religious service signifies moral redemption
although his impulses, represented by the heedless and talkative
people in the back of the room which symbolizes the back of
his mind, still bother and distract him. The distinction between
back and front in dreams has the same meaning as other such
spatial opposites as up and down, over and under, and right
and left. They usually refer to the higher and lower aspects of
man's nature.

His ambivalent feelings toward virtue, which is represented
by a church, is revealed in the next dream.

My buddy and I wanted to go swimming. In order to get the car
we had to go to church with my aunt. I think we had arrived at the

church when we decided that we couldn't go because we needed a shave and had no ties.

Swimming as noted before is a sensual activity, but before he can bathe in sensuality the dreamer feels that he should go to church. This is a curious turnabout in which redemption is sought before the sin has been committed. It is more typical for the revelry of Saturday night to be followed by expiation on Sunday morning. Some people, however, reverse the procedure. They are good in order that they can let themselves go later. In this dream the dreamer pictures himself as being so degraded that he is beyond redemption.

In this chapter we have observed some of the ways in which moral conflict expresses itself in dreams and some of the ways by which the dreamer tries to handle the conflict between impulse and conscience and alleviate his moral anxiety. It may have been noticed that most of the illustrative dreams used in this chapter are those dreamed by men. This selection was not intentional but is due to the fact that men seem to be more prone to have moral-conflict dreams than women do. This difference between the sexes does not result from men having more impulse expression in their dreams, for they do not, but the expression of impulses by men seems to arouse more anxiety. Women tend to be more realistic and less conscience-stricken. Does this mean that, on the whole, women have weaker consciences than men? We cannot say for sure, but the dreams of women certainly seem to suggest that this is the case.

We are quite certain, however, that the impulses of sex and aggression account for most if not all of the feelings of guilt experienced by people in dreams and probably in waking life as well. If this be true then man is certainly faced by a difficult problem. On the one hand these impulses are a part of his very nature and they will find ways of expressing themselves. If they cannot do it directly they will find indirect or covert ways, some of which are more harmful to society than a more direct expression would be. One thinks, for example, of the self-righteous person who expresses his hostility by punishing those who do not live up to his standards. Or one thinks of the sexually sadistic person who justifies his rapacious conduct by saying that "women like to be treated roughly." One thinks also of warmongers who would engage whole nations in war in order to satisfy their own pent-up aggression. The world is filled with such devious people.

On the other hand, society working through parental agents makes sure that these impulses will be curbed by implanting a conscience in the child. This conscience is equipped with rewarding and punishing mechanisms which it uses to keep the person in line with the dominant moral code of his society. Transgressions against the implanted morality of one's conscience are punished by making the person feel guilty, ashamed, remorseful and wicked. Nor does it do much good for one to behave properly since evil thoughts are as bad as evil deeds in the eyes of conscience and are punished as severely.

How then can man free himself from moral suffering? We leave the question unanswered. Perhaps man being man there is no answer.

9   The Conflict of Sex Roles

THE HUMAN family in common with other species is divided into two primary sex groups, male and female. From the moment of conception the maleness or femaleness of the newly conceived organism is laid down and no natural event thereafter can ordinarily alter it. Males never become females nor are females ever turned into males. This fixed and unalterable destiny of the individual is his *biological sex role.*

The biological role of the female is the bearing and rearing of offspring. In order to perform these functions, she is equipped with an *aperture*, the vagina, for the reception of the male germ cell, a *factory*, the ovaries, for the production of eggs, an *incubator*, the uterus, in which the unborn child resides and develops for nine months following conception, and *milk-giving* protuberances, the breasts, on which the baby is nourished until it is old enough to digest solid foods. These four physical structures, vagina, ovaries, uterus and breasts, characterize the female. However, structures by themselves cannot bear and rear children. Reproductive and maternal activities require participation by the whole individual. The adult female must *want* to mate and must *want* to take care of her young. These wants are psychological states. Their presence in the individual is not left to chance or to cultural training and education, but they are conditioned by two chemical substances called *hormones*, from a Greek word meaning *to excite*. Hormones are manufactured by the ovaries, deposited in the blood stream and circulated throughout the body. One of these hormones, the female sex hormone, is responsible for the female's desire to mate; the other, the maternal hormone, is responsible for the mother's urge to care for her young.

The sex role of the male, biologically speaking, is less complicated and less important than that of the female. He need perform only one function, that of providing the sperm to fertilize the egg; when that service is rendered he has fulfilled his biological destiny as a male. In order to discharge this function only two structures are needed, *a factory,* the testes, for the production of sperm, and a *protruding organ*, the penis, which will fit into the female aperture and discharge the germ cells. He must also want to perform the act of mating. The sexual impulse is conditioned by the male sex hormone, which is manufactured by the testes and discharged into the blood stream. There is no paternal hormone, because a father's care of the child is biologically unnecessary.

The sexes are also distinguished by other physical and psychological characteristics. Males are taller, heavier and more muscular, on the average, than females. The female tends to be round and soft, the male rectangular and hard. Males have tougher skins, hairier bodies, and deeper voices than females. Men tend to be more aggressive and women more submissive. The aggressiveness of the male is consistent with his greater bulk, his stronger muscles and his erectile, intrusive penis. The submissiveness of the female is in keeping with her smaller stature, her softness and her receptive sexual apparatus. One obvious psychological characteristic which distinguishes the sexes is that men tend to be attracted sexually to women and women tend to be attracted sexually to men. Were this not true, reproduction would be frustrated, and the species would soon die out. Sexual attraction between male and male and between female and female, that is, homosexuality, would obviously lead to the extinction of man. Heterosexuality is the biological norm.

In summary then, this is what it means to be a female. It means to have two external structures, vagina and breasts, and two internal organs, ovaries and uterus, a desire to mate with a man and an urge to nourish and rear children. It means being soft, smooth, passive and submissive.

This is what it means to be a male. It means having two visible organs, the penis and testes, and a desire to mate with a woman. It means being hard, rough, active and aggressive.

Culture exercises a considerable influence over the sex roles of males and females. What it means to be masculine or feminine differs from culture to culture, and within the same culture, prevailing conceptions of sex roles may not be the same for various communities, classes, and families. Even within a single family, parents may change their ideas about the kind of sex role they expect each child to assume. It is impossible, therefore, to generalize about cultural sex role norms without losing track of the individual case. It should be borne in mind, however, that cultural norms are always imposed upon individuals who possess definite biological and psychological characteristics.

The conflict of sex roles refers to the fact that both masculine and feminine characteristics are found within the same person, be he male or female, and that these characteristics contend with one another for expression. This internal conflict is fed from two sources, one cultural, the other biological.

Culture contributes to the conflict whenever it tries to force the individual to adopt a sex role that is at odds with his biological and psychological role as a male or female. Thus, if parents attempt to feminize the boy by deprecating masculinity, by denying him an opportunity to strengthen his muscles through exercise and rough games, and by encouraging him to be passive and obedient, they either invite trouble for themselves in the form of open rebellion or produce inward torment for the child by instilling habits contrary to his natural urges. Similarly, conflicts are aroused in girls by deprecating the visible emblems of femininity, by ridiculing such activities as playing with dolls, and by encouraging them to engage in strenuous muscle-building games and hard physical work. Any culture that favors one sex role over the other, as the middle class in the United States seems to prize masculine traits above feminine ones, is likely to reap a harvest of conflict.

On the biological side, the picture is complicated by a peculiar circumstance. It has been implied by what has been said that there is one biological and psychological role for males and one for females, and that each is separate and distinct from the other. This is not true. There are no such creatures as *pure* males or *pure* females, for *each sex manufactures some of the sex hormone of the opposite sex.* The male has some female sex hormone circulating in his blood, and the female has some male sex hormone circulating in her blood. Bisexuality and not unisexuality is the natural condition of man. The degree of bisexuality differs among individuals; a man may have much or little female hormone in proportion to male hormone and a woman may have much or little male hormone in proportion to female hormone. A male with a relatively high proportion of female hormone is more feminine in physique and temperament than one with a low proportion, and a woman with a relatively high proportion of male hormone is more masculine in physique and temperament than one with little male hormone. The fact that the ratio of the two hormones varies over a fairly large range means that there are many possible sexual gradations. Consider, for example, the gradations from the soft, flabby, hairless, high-voiced passive male to the hard, heavy-muscled, hairy, bass-voiced dominant male, and from the frail, ethereal female to the tough, aggressive amazon. Yet within each person of whatever gradation there exist masculine and feminine impulses. One part of the person is trying to be hard, active and aggressive, the other part is trying to be soft, passive and submissive. One part is attracted to members of the opposite sex and is heterosexual; the other part is attracted to members of the same sex and is homosexual. These two sides of man's nature are often at war with one another, and it is this struggle which we call the conflict of sex roles or simply the bisexual conflict.

Dreams offer a splendid opportunity to observe the bisexual conflict and the various ways in which a person tries to handle it. Occasionally we find dreams in which an actual sex reversal has taken place, as in the following dream of a young man.

I dreamed that I was lying in bed with white and red strips of cloth over me. Across my breasts the white strip stuck up as if I had female breasts. When I stood up the strips resolved themselves into a dress, and I did have breasts.

We happen to know from his other dreams and from additional sources of information that this lad has a strong bisexual conflict. He enjoys both homosexual and heterosexual outlets and is a curious mixture of feminine and masculine traits with passivity and self-love being his strongest features. At times he frankly admits that he would like to be a girl, and in this dream his wish is fulfilled. The white and red strips probably symbolize his conceptions of femininity and masculinity.

An example of sex reversal in women is seen in the next dream.

The main point of the dream is that there was a reversal of sexes. All of my girl friends were dressed as men and played the role of men while the men played the role of women.

This dream has the added feature of turning men into women as well as women into men, which suggests that not only does the dreamer want to be a man but also that she would like to get revenge on the dominant male by transforming him into the weaker sex.

One of the basic fears of young men is that they will lose their masculinity by being deprived of their sex organs. This is known as castration anxiety. It is caused by various factors, one of which is the bisexual conflict. A person who fears being emasculated actually wants to be turned into a woman but this wish runs counter to his opposite desire to be an adequate male. The consequence of this conflict is the same as that of all conflicts, namely, the person feels anxious.

Out-and-out dreams of castration are rare but not unheard of. One young man dreamed, for example, that a lion grabbed hold of his genitals and he awoke screaming. More often the idea of being castrated is represented in dreams by the loss of or injury to a part of the body other than the genital organs. The following dream of losing three teeth symbolizes castration.

I thought an upper tooth split in the middle and fell out with two others attached all in one solid piece. I held them between my fingers. Something resembling an inlay was attached to one of the teeth. It was long and protruded out of the bottom. It had a gold end sticking down into a lower tooth and when the tooth fell out a hole was left in this lower tooth.

The image of the three teeth with one tooth having something protruding from it resembles the male genital organs, and the hole that is left suggests the female genital organ. The dreamer has turned himself into a woman.

The idea of emasculation is also symbolized by loss or injury to a leg or arm. Dreams of losing a limb or having it damaged or incapacitated in some way are not uncommon. A young man dreamed, for example, that he was lying helpless on the floor while rats ate at his leg, while another man dreamed that a cat grabbed his leg.

Hair also is a symbol of manliness and its loss may signify castration. In this connection it will be recalled that Samson, the epitome of manly strength, lost his virility when Delilah cut off his long hair. Undue concern about the loss of hair is revealed in this dream.

I dreamed I was in a shower washing my hair. As I leaned my head forward and was rinsing the soap out I noticed that my head felt smooth. That is, it felt as though I had no hair at all on the top of my head. I couldn't believe it. I rushed to a mirror and sure enough all I had was about a two-inch strip along my forehead and along the sides of my head. Other than that I was bald. I showed my brother who thinks his hairline is receding and he just laughed. I then started a search for someone who could help me but I never found him.

This is the same dreamer who dreamed that rats were biting his leg and who also dreamed that he had lost his gun, which is a familiar masculine symbol.

A woman dreamer employed the symbolism of growing a beard to portray her wish to be a man.

I dreamed I was standing by a mirror with a friend of mine. I noticed a hair on my chin and on further investigation, discovered that I had grown a beard. The whole thing was very repulsive to me.

Her feeling of revulsion is a reaction against the fulfillment of her wish.

The thought of castration may also be represented by loss or destruction of objects which resemble the male member, such as a broken pencil, an uprooted tree, a squashed hat or a lost gun.

An unusual symbol for the loss of the badge of masculinity is contained in the following dream.

I was standing on top of a deep ravine watching the construction of a railroad bridge. The workmen were putting down the track and were using an engine and several cars to do it. The engine was pulling the cars and also the track and was about halfway across the bridge, when one of the cars caught on the end of the track and the engine pulled track and all out too far and all went plunging down to the bottom of the ravine.

This dreamer is known to be a chronic masturbator and his dream portrays the fear that masturbation will lead to the loss of masculinity. The engine stands for his sexual craving, while the track and cars which are pulled out too far and fall into a ravine represent the loss of his sexual organs. The same idea is presented in another one of his dreams.

I dreamed that we had a pretty bad storm and when I looked outside I saw a tree and limbs lying all over the ground. It seemed like a tornado or heavy wind had just tossed the trees around like toothpicks.

Here sexuality is represented by the bad storm and emasculation by the fallen trees. This dreamer's conception of castration as punishment for masturbation is fairly common among males, for it is not unusual for a boy to be told that his penis will be cut off or fall off if he plays with it.

Women also have castration dreams but the motivation for their dreams differs from that of men. They try to explain to themselves why they lack something which the male possesses.

In the following dream a woman is trying to account for her castrated condition.

I dreamed I was in a kitchen and heard some noises from the bedroom next to it as though someone were climbing in the window but I didn't bother to investigate. That night I went to bed and it seemed I was sleeping in a baby's bed with high sides and my sister was sleeping with her head at one end near the window and I had my head at the other side. When I woke in the morning I found I had been beaten up. I had bruises on my face and my right front tooth was broken and my left front tooth was missing. I didn't feel any pain but felt badly because my tooth was missing.

The loss of and damage to her teeth signify castration, an event that the dreamer imagines occurred during childhood since the dream is laid in that period of her life. Very likely she blames her sister with whom she is sleeping for beating her up and damaging her body although she does not come right out and say this in the dream.

Women often think of themselves as the castrated sex because they lack a prominent external member, and this conception of themselves not only makes them feel sad but also causes them to be envious of the better-equipped male. Her jealous feelings may motivate a woman to want to deprive men of their masculinity so that they will be castrated too. The picture of a grasping, castrating woman is clearly presented in this rather elaborate dream.

I was walking through a path in the woods with my mother. A man jumped out at us and held a gun at mother and demanded my purse. He was a complete stranger to me. I wanted to fight with him but mother held me back and told me to give him my purse. I asked him if I could just have the silver pencil which was in my purse, and give him the rest. He refused and I flung the purse on the ground and we walked on.

After a while I went back and saw a group of people sleeping on the ground. There was a pile of brown jackets on the green grass. I went through them all until I found the gun in the pockets of one of them. When I examined the gun, I found it to be a toy filled with caps which made noise when fired and had the odor of gunpowder. The thief was chagrined when he awoke and found out that I knew the gun was merely a toy, but he continued to act as if it were real. We struggled over possession of the gun, but I would not relinquish it. He left when he saw that I would not let him have it, and then I threw the gun on the ground and ran away.

In the first scene, she imagines that a man wants to take away her femininity, which is represented by a purse. He wants to rape her with his gun and when she tries to resist, her mother, who stands for the submissive side of the dreamer's nature, tells her to give in to the dominant male. The dreamer agrees to give him her purse if she can keep the silver pencil in it. The silver pencil is a male symbol and embodies the dreamer's conception of her masculinity. The first part of the dream says, in effect, "I will yield myself to a man if he will let me keep my masculinity." He refuses, which shows that the dreamer feels she has to submit completely to men by giving up everything upon demand.

In the second part of the dream she seeks revenge for the humiliation suffered in the first scene. Now she is going to emasculate the male by stealing his gun, but when she finds it, the gun turns out to be a mere toy. Thus she is able to deprecate masculinity and embarrass the man, which in itself is strong revenge. "Your vaunted masculinity is nothing but a toy." Still they fight over possession of this toy gun and the dreamer wins the contest. Once she has it, she throws it away. In the first scene, she rejects the feminine sex role, "I flung the purse on the ground," and in the second scene she rejects the masculine sex role, "I threw the gun on the ground." Neither role is satisfying in itself nor has she learned how to make her masculinity and femininity into a satisfying pattern of life. In this single dream the bisexual conflict unfolds itself in a most dramatic fashion.

Returning now to some male conceptions, we find that an important feature of a man's credo is that he shall be strong and virile. In his eyes weakness and impotence are feminine attributes and their presence in the picture he has of himself is apt to make him feel anxious. One young man's feeling of masculine inadequacy expresses itself in this way.

Indians were attacking my home; the setting except for the Indians was up-to-date. In order to protect the family I went out on the back porch with a large number of guns and began shooting at them. I was extremely frustrated because the bullets fell in front of me each time I fired, and I noticed that they were wooden bullets.

The gun and bullets are masculine symbols with which he tries to protect his family but his manliness is not equal to the task. Another dream reported by this dreamer conveys the same notion of his inadequacy as a male.

I was playing in the lot in back of our house and saw a rabbit and immediately gave chase. From nowhere there appeared a spear in my hand. I finally got the rabbit cornered and was about to plunge the spear into it, but couldn't because when I tried to throw it my arm wouldn't move. It just seemed numb.

He is so weak that he cannot even kill a rabbit let alone drive off hostile Indians. On the other hand, he invests women with masculine power as the next dream shows.

I dreamed that I met an old girl friend of mine. She was carrying a gun. I took the gun from her and tried it out, shooting at inanimate objects.

He does manage to assert his manhood by taking the gun away from her but instead of using it to shoot animals or enemies he tries it out on harmless inanimate objects. The idea of trying it out suggests the tentative character of this masculine self-assertiveness. Moreover, he has to borrow even this amount of manliness from a woman.

People who are in the grip of a strong bisexual conflict are constantly seeking ways to alleviate their anxiety. One favorite device that is widely used is to attack other people in whom one thinks he sees his own hated tendency. By doing this he not only attacks a part of his own make-up which he scorns, but he also tries to convince the world and himself that other men may have feminine characteristics but he certainly does not since he is so quick to punish others for having them. This is the motivation underlying the following dream of a man.

I was at the foot of some stairs and was told that there was someone on the second floor who was pregnant and that I must rush this person to the hospital. I had ridden to this building on a bicycle. I went upstairs and the only person I saw was a boy, two years older than I, that I vaguely knew at school. He said that it was he whom I was after. It made me furious and I shot him with a gun.

The dreamer is infuriated because a boy becomes pregnant and he destroys this feminine expression in a male by a ruthless display of masculine power. The dreamer is trying to root out his own femininity. This interpretation is borne out by another one of his dreams in which his homosexuality is clearly expressed.

I was kissing impassionately the lips of a male friend of mine and then going to sleep on his arm. No other portions of the body were involved. The identification of this friend was quite exact. He is my age and a buddy. I was quite conscious of his whiskers and his hair.

In commenting on this dream, the dreamer suggests that his boy friend is a substitute for his girl friend whom he has been neglecting because he has been spending most of his time with his buddy. Obviously he spends more time with the boy than with the girl because he likes him better than he likes her. His boy friend has displaced his girl friend in his thoughts. The homosexual conception of this dream is the same one he tries to destroy in the pregnancy dream.

Another way by which a person can defend himself against a shameful idea is to attribute the idea to another person and then have that person try to persuade the dreamer to do something which he wanted to do all along. The defending person can excuse himself by saying, "I couldn't help myself because he made me do it." This is the strategy employed by a young woman in the following dream.

I dreamed that a sorority sister of mine saw me in a movie theater and started to chase me throughout the theater. She was trying to seduce me and I did everything possible to avert her. I went up to several of my friends and told them that she was a homosexual. They refused to believe me and to help me get away from her. I started to leave the theater and she was sitting in the lobby reading a book. She did not see me walk out so I managed to get away from her.

The sorority sister personifies the dreamer's homosexuality, from which she tries to and finally does escape.

The tendency to recognize homosexual traits in others is usually an indication that the person himself is disturbed by his bisexuality. For example, a young man dreamed that someone showed him a copy of a newspaper.

The main story was an exposé of a boy who had been at summer camp and had slept in the same tent with me. The story in the emergency paper proved he was a homosexual.

This same young man also had a dream in which a man smiled at him in a homosexual way.

Moreover, the assumption that this dreamer leans toward homosexuality is supported by a dream in which he has a date with a female usher who is reputed to be a whore.

I am overcome with tenderness for her. I think she is wearing her usher's uniform and I noticed she was flat-breasted. We admire with poetic sensitivity the sea. I ask her whether I might kiss her. She said she did not mind but told me she was incapable of passion. I did not mind too much.

He masculinized the girl by having her wear a uniform and appear flat-breasted. He does not mind her being without passion because this saves him from the anxiety he might feel should they become more sensual. In his next dream, he exaggerates the size of a woman's breasts rather than minimizing them as in the former dream.

She had small pointed breasts with tremendous nipples. I knew she was engaged and I thought of her fiancé sucking the nipples. I thought if he can do it, so can I.

At first glance this dream seems to be one of regression to an infantile state when the dreamer derived pleasure from nursing at his mother's breast. Yet one is struck by the peculiar description of the breasts, "small pointed breasts with tremendous nipples." These nipples are shaped more like the male genital organ than like normal breasts. If this is the case, then the dreamer is expressing a desire to engage in oral sexuality.

In another dream he is making love to a girl when his buddy enters

and started laughing cynically. He called the girl hard-up. She started to cry. I was angry at my boy friend.

In this dream he casts doubts on his own manliness. The perception of others as homosexual, the masculinizing of women and a sense of his own inadequacies as a man reveals the pattern of this dreamer's bisexual conflict.

In the next example of a person defending himself against his own homosexual inclinations the dreamer accuses his girl of being a homosexual.

My fiancée was getting a physical examination at her doctor's office. She was standing nude before her doctor, a woman, who was thumping her chest. The doctor then had her recline on the

couch and administered a hypodermic in her left buttock. The effect
of the shot made her unconscious. The doctor was undressed herself now and engaged in sexual relations with her.

This is an interesting departure from the more familiar projection of homosexuality onto a person of the same sex, although
its meaning is very much the same with possibly one exception.
If one's girl friend has sexual relations with other women then
it is all right for the man to have relations with other men. It
is just another kind of self-justification.

In commenting upon this dream the dreamer says that the
office reminded him of his own doctor's office. Since his physician is a man this comment suggests that the dreamer harbors
a desire to be treated by him as his girl is treated by her physician.
In another dream of this young man his girl snubs him for
another girl.

I brought a girl to the movie but lost her just after entering.
I was riding around on my bicycle looking for my date. I found
her, sat next to her, and then I asked her to move so that we could
see the screen better. She refused because there was a girl next to
whom she wanted to sit. I felt snubbed.

His comment upon this dream is that his girl may be a Lesbian
because of her close attachment to her mother. This comment
suggests another interpretation, namely, that he has homosexual
leanings because of a close identification with his mother. It
should be pointed out in this connection that attachment to and
identification with are quite different matters. An attachment
means "I like so-and-so" while an identification means "I am
like so-and-so." A boy who is attached to his mother is displaying
a perfectly normal heterosexual interest while a boy who is

identified with his mother has taken over a feminine conception of himself.

The dreams of young men are filled with scenes of masculine camaraderie and this camaraderie is not without overtones of sensuality. At such times when men are enjoying each other's companionship, their rivalry and competition as males are pushed into the background while their affection for one another takes the center of the stage. They play games, swim, drink beer, hunt and fish or just relax in each other's company as the following dream illustrates.

I dreamed that my boy friend and I had just completed a day at college. It was a beautiful summerlike day so we walked all around the park. The stroll was very peaceful and there were no outstanding events.

What a contrast between the peaceful quality of this dream and the dissension that occurs when a girl enters his dream.

I dreamed that I was out on a date with a girl friend enjoying a pleasant evening. As we were talking an argument arose which became very heated, and finally she started slapping me, which infuriated me, and I threw her out of the car.

Another dreamer who has had a fight with a girl meets a buddy.

My anxious feeling was relieved when I recognized an old friend of mine and was able to share his companionship.

Men who served in World War II frequently dream of being back in service with their friends, and these dreams are not anxious war dreams but pleasant images of masculine companionship which for many men constituted the attractive side of military service. Men without women or women without men can be very happy in dreams. The following dream was reported by a veteran.

There was a knock at the door. I went and answered it. It was an old Navy buddy from Michigan. He had his uniform on. I asked what he was doing back in uniform. He then handed me a slip of paper. The paper ordered me back to active duty immediately. So I put on my uniform, packed my gear and left with my buddy.

The dreamer, who is married and attends school, shows by this dream that he would rather be back in service with his buddy. This interpretation is corroborated by his other dreams. In one he and a friend are back in the Navy stationed together on a small island, while in another he re-enlists in the Navy. In a third dream one of his old shipmates visits him and in a fourth he and a companion share a foxhole together.

The tender regard that a man has for another man or a woman for another woman should not be regarded as a direct expression of sexuality. Rather it signifies a sublimation of sexual impulses. By sublimation is meant that erotic energy has been diverted from the goal of sexual discharge to the goal of affectionate friendship. Handclasps and embraces are substituted for sexual relations. Camaraderie becomes an end in itself. Sublimated sexuality is the theme of many of Walt Whitman's poems, but in none has it been more beautifully portrayed than in this one.

For the one I love most lay sleeping by me under the same cover in the cool night,
In the stillness, in the autumn moonbeams, his face was inclined toward me,

And his arm lay lightly around my breast—and that night I was
   happy.

Women have more opportunity for affectionate contacts with
each other than men do because their embraces and kisses are
not frowned upon by society. Tenderness is the essence of femininity. Moreover, women are permitted to behave in masculine
ways to a far greater extent than men are permitted to behave in
feminine ways. When women wear trousers and shirts nobody
pays much attention, but let a man appear in a dress and he
becomes the object of ridicule and contempt. This trivial illus-
tration explains why men suffer more anxiety from the bisexual
conflict than women do and why they dream about it more often.

Tenderness between males arouses anxiety when it becomes
too blatant, in which case affection is replaced by anger, handclasps by blows, and embraces by fighting. Imagine the following
scene which might take place almost any Saturday night in a
neighborhood bar. The tavern is filled with a number of men
and a few women. Many of the men are congregated at the bar,
swapping stories, singing songs, throwing their arms over one
another's shoulders and slapping each other affectionately, as
they propose sentimental toasts. There they stand making a
pleasant picture of masculine camaraderie. Suddenly the mood
of the group changes. Someone takes offense at a chance remark
or a fancied insult. In a moment, love turns into hate, smiling
faces become hostile masks, open hands are doubled into angry
fists, a blow is struck and the congenial fraternity becomes a
fighting mob. Bottles are thrown, mirrors and windows are
broken, tables and chairs are overturned. Someone draws a knife

and blood begins to flow. Finally the police are called to quell the riot. By this time, the fighting and bloodshed have served the purpose of expunging the feminine impulse of tenderness which had become too open in its expression. The men are able to say, "We are tough, combative males, not soft tender women."

Men who reject any sign of softness in their character, who view tenderness between males as an alien danger, and who look upon homosexuality as a vicious perversion are apt to defend themselves against their femininity by exaggerated aggressiveness and violence. They see the world as an armed camp and a battlefield in which man contends with man and nation with nation. Their vision is distorted by hatred of their own femininity and their world outlook is a bastion against their own homosexuality.

This view of the world is portrayed in the dream series of a young veteran. He dreams he is back in combat with his buddies.

We passed a group of enemy soldiers who were firing a huge gun, and when we passed they laughed and waved and said they were just practicing.

The dual conception of men as buddies and men as enemy soldiers is manifested in this part of the dream. By investing the enemy with a huge gun the dreamer says in effect that their masculinity is superior to his, but he avoids feeling anxious by having the enemy appear friendly. Then he finds himself in an enemy house preparing to go to bed with one of his buddies when they are interrupted by the appearance of two other soldiers, closely followed by two young women. The women ask the dreamer to take them dancing but he refuses.

I was ashamed that I had only my dirty uniform to wear, and as I do not like dancing, I used the fact that I had no new suit as an excuse for not taking them to the dance.

Here we see a transition from homosexuality, going to bed with a buddy, to heterosexuality, going to a dance with two women. He rejects the invitation to heterosexuality by refusing to take them dancing. However, his heterosexuality is not so easily put off since the girls suggest they might as well all go to bed and proceed to disrobe.

I took one of them into bed with me and began to have intercourse with her, although I seemed to have a great deal of difficulty in the act.

Even so the dreamer has difficulty in playing the male role and the dream does not end with a nocturnal emission as might be expected.

In another dream a buddy and a girl compete for his affection. As the dream opens he is riding in an automobile with his boy friend when suddenly his girl appears and sits in his arms.

We were still in my friend's car and he was smiling and talking to us. I began to pet with my girl, and I told her of my love for her and how much I wanted to marry her. She was smiling and very happy and began to kiss me and I began to want her by intercourse. Before I could hold her, I woke up.

Although his buddy encourages the dreamer's heterosexuality by smiling and talking to them, sexual union is not achieved. In a third dream he and his Army friends are reunited as members of the National Guard, a situation that causes the dreamer to be happy because he is with his old friends and to be anxious because of the feminine implications of this comradeship.

Active combat with the enemy is the theme of two dreams. In one of these he is in a foxhole with two other men when he is ordered to leave the foxhole, kill an enemy soldier with his bare hands and return with a new type of gun which is wanted by army intelligence. This dream symbolizes the dreamer's concern over his inadequate masculinity and his desire to improve it by wresting an emblem of virility away from another man. Moreover, by castrating another male, his own masculinity will appear to be enhanced.

The second combat dream causes him great anxiety because the superior force of a masculine enemy is clearly apparent.

I was in the rear and when I came upon the company they were hidden around a hill and nearby an enemy gun was being fired. I came upon the company and the leader whispered to be quiet and not to shoot because if the enemy on the gun saw us we would be shot to pieces. Suddenly a man next to me began to struggle with an enemy soldier and began to choke him. Suddenly firing broke out and I had an almost overwhelming impulse to run but only ran a few feet and then laid flat on the ground with another soldier.

In this dream the enemy is not friendly nor is it merely practicing with its superior equipment as it was in a former dream. The dominant note here is the dreamer's fear of the enemy and his unmanly desire to run away.

The hostility of the dreamer toward both sexes is brought out in the next dream.

I was out west and went into a bar. A stranger came up and started to fight with me. I fought back. The scene shifted and there were a number of young women around me. I became enraged and yelled that I would shoot them. I pulled out a revolver and began to shoot at them, but the bullets only floated out of the gun and did not hurt them. Then the women began to laugh and I gave up trying to hurt them and walked away.

The double-barreled hostility in this dream is an ambitious attempt on the part of the dreamer to remove any doubts about his masculinity. Following a fight with a man, he turns his aggression against women, who represent the feminine side of his character. However, he cannot maintain a self-conception of virility since the bullets merely float out of his gun and do no harm. Finally he gives up trying to destroy his femininity.

Our dreamer's lack of masculinity makes him feel inferior in sexual competition with other men. In one dream he is riding in an automobile with two other men and a girl whom he does not see very clearly although he thinks it is his girl. He accuses one of the other passengers of stealing her away from him, which is denied. When the dreamer is able to see the girl's face he discovers she is not his girl although there is some resemblance. This dream ends happily. In another dream he actually loses his girl to another man, which leaves him with feelings of anger, fear, jealousy, sorrow and a profound sense of his own impotence. He seeks his revenge in another dream by making love to a buddy's girl.

This young man's perplexity about his sex role has its origins in the family circle. Older men are pictured both as friends and as enemies. In one dream a good father helps him to get into medical school, while in another dream he is attacked by a group of bad fathers. Having mixed feelings about older men, it might be expected that the dreamer has had a hard time making a good identification with his father. It must be remembered that the father is the first model of masculinity for the boy.

Moreover, the dreamer is the youngest of five children, a circumstance that provides an opportunity for a person to develop feelings of inferiority. He dreams that his brothers and sisters berate him roundly for smashing up his car, to which he replies that he does not care whether he destroys it or not. Since an automobile is usually a symbol of masculine power, this dream signifies that he is not concerned about maintaining his masculinity, although actually he is terribly worried about it.

How will the conflict turn out? Although we cannot be certain, his dreams do contain some hints of the course he is trying to follow. In one dream he is an Army officer and eats with the general. Here he is trying to attain masculinity by identifying with a dominant male. In another dream he is crossing a bridge with some other young men. It begins to hail and the other boys withdraw, leaving the dreamer alone on the bridge.

I was caught on the bridge and was undecided which way to go as I was afraid I would be hurt by the stones. The others yelled at me that I would get hurt so I rushed back across the bridge and ducked into a small shed in which there was a colored gas station attendant.

While he is trying to make a transition in his life he becomes frightened and unsure of himself and returns to safety. In another dream he is running down an endless country lane flanked by tall trees.

As I sped down the road people appeared, mostly middle-aged people who smiled as I flashed past. I smiled also but no words of greeting were exchanged. I began to run faster and faster and suddenly the effort of running began to tell and I began to breathe hard. The scene faded and I slowed down.

Running but never arriving is this young man's conception of his life. He would like to be a confident, effective male but feelings of impotence prevent this self-picture from developing.

We must bring this chapter to a close although a great deal more might be said about the dynamics of human bisexuality. The conflicts and anxiety that it engenders, the numerous ways by which people try to relieve their apprehensiveness, and the official and unofficial attitudes of society toward deviations from the conventional sex roles of male and female deserve more attention than we have been able to give them. We have seen that dreams can and do supply us with many insights concerning the nature of this basic and pervasive human predicament.

10   Life Versus Death

AS ONE grows older a new shadow falls over the mind of man. It is the shadow of physical and mental disintegration. The ebb of life gradually but relentlessly overtakes and passes the flow of life. One day the person realizes that he is no longer young, later he acknowledges that he is getting old, and finally he admits that he is ready to die. Inevitable as death is, man does not yield submissively to his own disintegration. While there is still some life energy left, he fights off death, and it is this struggle between life and death which constitutes the principal conflict of man's later years. In a sense the struggle has been going on since the moment of conception, but it is not until man has passed the halfway mark of his life that the two adversaries become more equally matched. Before this time the reservoir of life energy is usually sufficient to meet any demands that are made upon it. As the energy dissipates, the shadow of death grows longer, until it envelops the person.

The struggle between life and death, like the other basic conflicts of man, does not ordinarily display itself in public. Its arena is located in the deeper recesses of the mind, where it cannot be seen by the person himself, let alone by others: However, when the more superficial layers of the mind are asleep, thoughts emanate from these farther corners in the form of dreams. Hence, if we want to observe the conflict between life and death we must explore the dreams of older people. This is what we intend to do in the present chapter.

We start out with a series of dreams of a man in his sixty-eighth year who recently had quit work because of ill health. Prior to his illness he had lived an active life, worked hard, participated in community and church activities, and engaged in such outdoor pursuits as hunting, fishing and gardening. His life now seems to be drawing to a close. Does he give in gracefully to this new state of affairs? Not at all, as the following dream reveals.

I found myself walking with a lovely lady about twenty-five years of age. The scene shifted to a night club where a festive time was enjoyed drinking and dancing. The scene shifted again to a cool stream and we plunged in. I swam effortlessly, sliding and gliding through the water like a fish. All of a sudden my lady friend vanished. An unknown man watching from the bank complimented me on my swimming prowess and I replied, "Others may be younger and stronger but I still can outswim them all."

He dreams of the restoration of his virility which is represented by a variety of sensual settings and activities. Yet in spite of his apparent rejuvenation he has to acknowledge that "others may be younger and stronger." This is the dream of an older person who strenuously resists the thought of his own dissolution.

In another dream he returns to the country where he was born and raised.

I dreamed I was back in Jugoslavia, the land of my youth. I am waiting for a train. The train comes along, rolling swiftly. I attempt to catch it, but fall back afraid I may not be able to grab hold. The train stops momentarily but speedily rolls away again before I can board it. I continue on, wading through water until I come to a flour mill. I see large fish in the water and think that it is probably good fishing there. I walk on.

The train represents the forward-going vector of youth which the dreamer tries to recapture unsuccessfully. Life passes him by because he no longer has the agility to seize and hold it. Undaunted he continues his search for youthful vitality, which is symbolized by the water, the flour mill and the thought of good fishing in a stream where there are so many large fish.

The foregoing dream is laid in the land of his youth and this feature marks it as a regressive dream. Many of the dreams of older people, as we shall see, look backward in time to contrast with the dreams of younger people, which are oriented toward the present or the future. Obviously if an older person desires rejuvenation he has to return to an earlier period of his life. Moreover, going backward in time takes him further away from life's end, the thought of which may cause him considerable anguish.

In the next dream our dreamer relives a hunting experience.

I dreamed I was in a wooded area hunting for rabbits. I was accompanied by a good friend and hunting companion of the past.

A rabbit jumped out of the brush and I shouted to my partner. He shot and missed. I shot and the rabbit went down. "It's yours," I said. "You shot first." But he refused to take it so I retrieved the rabbit. We met another acquaintance who said he had to go home and get some wine. I told him to go ahead as we didn't intend to stay much longer.

The dreamer's favorite pastime before his illness was hunting. He took great pride in his marksmanship and liked to boast about beating his hunting companions to the kill. A drinking bout usually followed a hunting trip. This dream like the first two takes him back to the good old days when he was alert and strong and competitive. However, the dream does not end here but continues on a back-to-work theme.

The scene shifted suddenly to my bedroom. I awoke (in the dream) with the realization that I was late for work. I hurried into my clothes and dashed for the streetcar. I couldn't seem to make the proper connections and took another car which left me some distance from the shop. It was time for the whistle and I began to run so as not to be late to work. As I am running, I awoke.

This transition from the pleasures of hunting and drinking to the worry of getting to work on time is a logical one because if he were able to hunt he would also be able to work. His concern does not arise from the thought of being late but rather of not being able to return to work at all because of his advanced years and ill health. He realizes what the obstacles are, for he dreams that he could not make the proper connections and boards a streetcar that carries him away from the shop. Even in his dreams he is realistic enough to recognize that there is little chance of his either hunting or working again. A conception of youthfulness is at odds with a conception of agedness in this dream, and age wins out.

Before his incapacitation the dreamer had been active in the social life of his church, having been in charge of the annual church picnic. The following dream occurred during the night before this event, which the dreamer was going to miss for the first time in his adult life because of his illness.

I found myself in a parish church sitting in a side pew. Two men came up and asked me to take up the collection. I replied, "You tell the priest at the altar to do the collecting, not I." I then found myself outside the church listening to a men's choir that was singing in front of the church. The strains of the organ resounded beautifully. A man came up to me and said, "If you didn't lead the choir so well, the singing would not be so beautiful." An old man came down the steps at this time and walked through a window of an adjoining house. I turned to the group and remarked that it would be good to have a drink. Three ladies escorted us to the adjoining school house where they served whiskey. As I stood there with money in my hand about to pay, I awoke.

Although there are regressive features in this dream, such as leading the choir and drinking, the dominant orientation is one of recognizing present realities. He sees himself sitting in a side pew which indicates that he has been relegated to the side line of life, and he refuses to take up the collection which signifies withdrawal from church activities. The appearance of an old man personifies the dreamer's conception of himself and his walking through a window is a way of saying that he is bowing out of the picture. Nonetheless the dreamer rejects this conception of himself and suggests they all have a drink. The literal meaning of the word whiskey is water of life and the drinking of it is therefore a splendid symbol of rejuvenation. In fact most people drink in order to feel more lively. However, the fact that the dreamer awakens before he can pay for the drinks shows that his wish for rejuvenation cannot be fulfilled.

The main theme of the preceding dreams is the opposition between a conception of rejuvenation and a conception of disintegration. The next dream introduces new material concerning the nature of this conflict and the kind of solution he proposes to make.

I dreamed I was in a wooded area. Then the scene shifted to an old brick house, several stories high. I was in one of the top rooms, which was lined with bookshelves. A woman about thirty years old was sorting and dusting the books. A man of about the same age was also present. They paid no attention to me. I warned the young woman that the books contained war bonds and she should be careful what she does with them, that they represent a great deal of money and I want them properly cared for. The scene shifts to the basement of the building, which resembled a foundry. Another man and woman in their late twenties were there. They appeared indifferent to me. I complained that I was not being treated with the proper respect and consideration. I asked about the whereabouts of my mother and they replied they did not have any knowledge of her whereabouts.

The old brick house represents the dreamer's conception of himself, while the activity of the woman dusting and arranging the books suggests the sort of thing that goes on after a person dies. This interpretation is supported by the dreamer's warning that she should be careful of the books because they contain valuable bonds and he wants them taken care of properly. This is just what one might say to one's heirs. The young man and woman stand for his son and daughter-in-law with whom he lives and to whom presumably he will leave his money. However, he feels neglected by them and they do not even respect him for his money, which is the only valuable possession he has left. In this connection it is interesting that money seems to take on added significance as one grows older. It represents a store of energy for the old person and that is why he husbands it so carefully. The frugality of old age is caused by a general concern over the dissipation of energy.

The shift in scene from a top room in a house to a basement symbolizes a change in the direction of his thought from the present to the past, from that which is uppermost in his mind to that which is buried deep in his memories. As he retreats into the past it is natural for him to think of his mother. She will give him love and consideration which he is not getting from his son and daughter-in-law. But his mother is dead and the only way he can find her is to join her in death. Although he cannot bring himself to think of his own death, the idea exists implicitly in his thoughts and offers a solution to his conflict. As he grows still older we can predict that this solution will become more attractive to him, for death is conceived of by many old people not as the end of everything but as the beginning of a new life with one's parents, friends and relatives long since dead. This is the view of death held by most religions.

Another series, this one collected from a woman of fifty-five illustrates further the struggle between life and death. Her first dream is a lovely image of the simple pleasures enjoyed by children.

I dreamed I was a child again and was walking with my best girl friend over a trail. It had just rained and the water was in rivulets and pools. We lay down and began to collect smooth round pebbles. Then suddenly we were gathering sea shells on a seashore—all different kinds of shells. Then the scene changed again to one full of peeping, yellow, newly-hatched chicks.

One can almost smell the fresh, rain-washed woods, feel the smooth, glistening pebbles, and see the downy yellow chicks in this pre-eminently regressive dream. The newly-hatched chicks are a particularly appropriate symbol of rebirth, for the hatching of chicks is an emblem of that great period of nature's reawakening, Eastertide.

Another excursion back to childhood is depicted in the following dream.

I dreamed I was a little girl playing on our front yard, when my favorite uncle surprised us by an unannounced visit. He kissed me and I felt his stubby beard and noticed the gold pince-nez which he wore. He showed my mother a picture of his wife, only he said it wasn't a picture but actually his wife. I could hardly wait to show him my school grades for he always asked to see them. Suddenly I became frightened because I didn't know the Pythagorean theorem. But this fear quickly passed and I was happy again.

This happy re-enactment of a childhood memory is marred briefly by the dreamer's inability to remember the Pythagorean theorem in geometry. The reader will recall that this theorem states that in a right triangle, the square on the longest side equals the sum of the squares on the other two sides. Does this mean that the dreamer feels anxious because she is reminded of a human triangle in which she once figured? The presence of an affectionate uncle and the intrusion of his wife suggests such an interpretation. There are problems in childhood, too, which one encounters in fleeing from present problems.

The next dream is also regressive.

I dreamed that I was walking to school with my girl friend. We were discussing the coming exam, and we hoped we wouldn't get asked a certain difficult question. When we got to school, my girl friend was stuck with this tough question. I felt happy and sad at the same time.

In this dream the dreamer uses a common stratagem of passing off a difficult problem on someone else. This is what she would like to do with her present problem.

Another happy recollection of the good times of youth is found in the following dream, although the small cloud of fear and sadness which has been gathering in the last two dreams becomes more menacing in this one.

I dreamed I was eighteen again and four couples of us were on a moonlight ride in a boat. The night was dark, it was after midnight, the water clear, quiet and cold. Nearby was "Nightingale Island." On it, high on the trees, nightingales sang beautiful songs. We were all happy and shouting.

Suddenly a boat approached contained four villains. It came closer, closer. We all became very frightened, filled with dread. Suddenly the boats touched and I felt one of the strangers grab me. He said, "Come with us!" We became even more frightened. Then our boy friends and the strange men were fighting. We frightened girls didn't know what to do, whether try to swim back to shore or stay.

The menacing cloud in this dream turns out to be the dreamer's fantasy of being raped. This fantasy in which sexual conquest is conceived of as a violent abduction by villainous males is quite common in the dreams of younger women, and it represents for this dreamer one of the hazards of returning to her earlier life. In other words, the good old days had their bad ones, too. One pays a price for regression.

The preceding four dreams of this series were laid in childhood and adolescence. The next dream takes her back to the early days of her married life.

I was walking along a familiar street pushing a buggy. The birds were singing and the sky was bright blue. The baby was one of my sons. He was already old enough to walk but because I was going some distance, the baby sat in the buggy. I felt happy as I strolled and told nursery rhymes to my child.

While all was happy and bright, I suddenly realized that the sky was getting stormy and dark. I became filled with uneasiness and wanted to reach home before the storm broke. I hurried but it seemed even longer to my home. During this time my baby listened enraptured to the rhymes, even those he had heard before. Finally I reached home and was glad. But the door was locked and I could not get inside. Then I awoke.

She is reliving the pleasures of motherhood, when the sky which has been bright and sunny becomes dark and cloudy. She hurries to get back to the security of her home before the storm breaks but when she arrives there the door is locked and she cannot get in. What she is saying in this dream is that there is no escape from the gathering storm of her present life. It is closing in on her, and in the next dream it breaks out in all its fury.

I was looking for a hotel room in Florida. I was shown many rooms by the clerk but I wanted to see more. Finally he showed me a big pleasant room with a large bed. Through the wide window I could see the red rosy sunset. I asked the attendant if the hotel was noisy.

Suddenly the attendant disappeared and the sky outside darkened and became green, black and yellow. The weather was very hot and a cool sandstorm was upon me. My eyes were filled with sand and more and more sand filled the room. The drapes and Venetian blinds fell off and it got cooler. The nice large bed, a picture and lamp were swirling around in the windswept room. I saw two clouds in the room, one cold and sandy, the other warm. Outside, the green, blue and red lights of the miniature golf course danced in front of my eyes. The parked cars below swam in the storm.

Then the clerk reappeared as the storm subsided and I asked, "Is this a small storm?" The clerk said no. Then another sandstorm started. This was really a big storm. The clerk was sunburned red with red hair.

What does this storm represent? She tells us that it is a cool sandstorm, and that as it progresses her room becomes cooler, finally turning quite cold. Before the storm begins she is in a big pleasant room in a warm, sunny climate and it is this setting which is destroyed by the sandstorm. The real meaning of the dream is found in the sentence, "I saw two clouds in the room, one cold and sandy, the other warm." These two clouds represent two conflicting conceptions of herself. One conception is that of a cold, frigid woman whose sensual vitality and power have disappeared with advancing years. The other conception is that of a warm, passionate person who can still find much pleasure in life. The clerk in the dream represents her husband, who actually has red hair. His disappearance as the storm starts and his reappearance as the storm subsides indicates that he is a symbol of life. The dream ends pessimistically with the start of another larger storm.

A more optimistic dream is the next one.

I was being driven home from downtown by a lady in a new car. We were so engrossed in a pleasant conversation we passed my home and found ourselves driving by green fields, perhaps a golf course.

Suddenly the scene changed and there were a crowd of people on horses. Everyone was shouting and yelling. Although there was a yellow dust in the air, my vision was clear. I found myself among the people on horses. There were mostly men in the crowd.

The new car, the green field, the people on horseback, and the shouting and yelling represent vitality and fertility. The horse, it will be recalled, is a favorite embodiment of the conception of unbridled sexuality. It will be noted, however, that there is a little yellow dust in the air but not enough to blot out the picture of rejuvenation which is in her mind.

The rabbits in the following fecund dream also symbolize the return of her fertility.

I dreamed I awoke one morning, went downstairs and looked out the back door. I saw an animal and at first I thought it was a rat, but it turned out to be a large rabbit. The rabbit came up to the doorway and looked at me. I wanted to get a carrot for the rabbit. When I looked again there were two rabbits, then three, four—until the whole yard was filled with rabbits. They began to eat the carrot. I did not feel afraid but was pleased to see all the tame rabbits. I made plans to feed them during the cold winter.

Nonetheless she cannot avoid thinking of the long winter of sterility that lies ahead of her.

The last dream of her series is singularly profound.

I dreamed I was in the elevator of my hotel. The elevator opened onto the solarium facing the Miami beach. The elevator was closed and moving but I was afraid that I had pressed the wrong button. I was alone in the elevator, which was self-operating. I wanted to go up to my room to change my clothes because it was very hot. I was frightened because the elevator was going down. It stopped but the door would not open. In panic I yelled and knocked but no one came. Time seemed an eternity. I forgot where I was, down or up, and I did not know what to do.

Suddenly I was free of the elevator and green foamy waves were rolling over me. I felt refreshed, my mind clear. I thought surely someone will come and open the elevator. The waves rose higher and filled my eyes and nose. I thought, "Who can resist such tremendous waves?" I forgot about the elevator and the waves became all-important. Time passed very slowly. The recurring waves were not so bad. They refreshed me. I thanked God that I was heavy so that the waves could not carry me away. I recalled the various ways of reducing that I had tried. I was not far from shore. Finally the waves broke over me and I saw the dim outline of the shore. I felt safe. I realized that the elevator door would open up.

The desire to go up to her room represents the ascension or life conception but the fact that she is in a small elevator tells us that her present life is a constricted one. She pushes the wrong button and the elevator goes down rather than up. Then it stops and she cannot get out. What does this whole scene suggest? It suggests death and burial. The elevator is a coffinlike container from which there is no escape. In her dream, time seemed an eternity just as it would in death.

Suddenly the scene changes and she is in the water, free of
the elevator. She feels refreshed and although the waves rise
higher and higher she thinks, "Who can resist such tremendous
waves?" Finally she sees the dim outline of the shore and feels
safe.

What does all this mean? She dies but what does death mean?
It means returning to the great ocean from which all life sprang.
Walt Whitman has likened the sea to a cradle endlessly rocking.

> Whereto answering, the sea,
> Delaying not, hurrying not,
> Whisper'd me through the night, and
>   very plainly before daybreak,
> Lisp'd to me the low and delicious word DEATH.

Death is a delicious word for our dreamer as well as for Walt
Whitman because it means rebirth into a new spacious world.
Death is not a coffin, it is the great wide sea.

This then is her conflict as her dreams formulate it. "I do not
want to grow old and sterile. I want to be young again and enjoy
the passion of youth. However, I realize that this is impossible.
Moreover, to relive my life would mean to relive old conflicts
that once caused me so much grief. I cannot go back to what
I once was. I cannot go ahead to what I want to be." Still in her
dreams she tries to resolve this most profound of all human
tragedies.

The foregoing dream has the comic relief of all great literature. While the waves are rolling over her she thanks God that
her attempts to reduce have not been successful and that she
is heavy enough to resist the death-bringing waves. After all
there is some compensation for being overweight.

The struggle between the tensions of life and death has been clearly portrayed in the preceding dream series of a man in his sixties and a woman in her fifties. In the next series, obtained from a married woman of forty-five who has two children, a son and a daughter in their early twenties, the opposing tensions of life and death have not reached a climax. The life urge is still in the ascendance although the forebodings of declining years appear in her dreams. She is beginning to think of herself as an old woman whom life is passing by.

In one of her dreams she is walking through the dark, dingy corridors of an old building whose offices are occupied by doctors and beauty parlors. No one pays any attention to her and she cannot find her way out of the building. The image which the dreamer has of herself is embodied in the setting of the dream. Visits to doctors and beauty parlors are the lot of middle-aged women who are trying to stave off the ravages of age. They feel ignored and they would like to find their way out of the dark, dingy corridors of advancing years.

In another dream she and another woman are in a dining room waiting to be served. "A dozen waitresses passed but no one waited on us. Try as we might we could not get service." In desperation the dreamer does something drastic in the third dream of her series in order to secure attention. "I walked along the street stark naked." Yet even this strategy is unsuccessful because her husband and other people on the street appeared indifferent to her lack of attire. No one will pay any attention to her.

In several dreams she tries to appropriate her daughter's boy friend. For example she dreams that he is giving her a number of presents. When the dreamer opens them they turn out to be cheap, ugly lamps which are abhorrent to her. This solution to her problem does not work because she realizes how dishonest it is of her to try to win a young man's love, much as she might like to.

Finally this frustrated, middle-aged woman walks back over the path of her life until she meets someone who will pay attention to her and love her as he once did.

I dreamed of my father who has been dead for twenty-five years. I had a feeling of well-being and was not at all conscious of the fact that he was dead. I made applesauce for him because he always liked it so much. Next he played music but I am vague as to what the piece was or how it was being played.

She tells us that this is a recurring dream and whenever she dreams it she feels very happy. Others may ignore her and spurn her love but her father is an ever faithful lover to whom she can go for comfort and consolation.

This dream also embodies the notion of death since she joins her father who has been dead for a long time. She tries to deny this implication by saying she was not conscious of his being dead. However, it is evident that to dream of a dead person, even though the dreamer may summon the person back to life, means that the conception of death is in the mind of the dreamer. The wish for death as a solution to the problems of life may not be as strong in a person who has this type of dream but it is beginning to stir.

Dreaming of people who are dead may take various forms, depending upon the conception which the dreamer has of death. A middle-aged woman whose husband had died recently dreamed that he got in touch with her by telephone. The radio was playing so loudly that the dreamer could not hear him and when she returned to the phone after turning it off he was no longer on the line. "I begged the operator to give me a better connection but it had been broken. I was crying and crying and said, 'Now I can never find him. I don't know where he is.'" This dreamer's conception of death is that it is a broken connection between people.

Another woman whose husband had been dead for two years had this dream.

I was in the middle of a crowd and it seemed like a cocktail party, when all of a sudden I saw my husband. He didn't see me but instead started to walk away. I called out to him by name and asked him to wait for me. I yelled so loudly that I woke myself.

Here there is an active wish to join her husband, although her strenuous yelling which awakens her suggests that she is having some trouble trying to realize this wish. The trouble, of course, arises from the fact that her desire for death is counteracted by a life wish.

Sometimes death is conceived of as a summons given to a dreamer by a dead relative. A fifty-five-year-old woman dreamed that her father who had been dead for fourteen years came into the room where the dreamer was lying on the davenport, touched her hand for a moment without saying anything and then walked out of the room. The touch suggests that the father is inviting the dreamer to follow him.

Another conception of death is portrayed in the next dream reported by a middle-aged woman.

I saw a very old woman who resembled my grandmother dressed in black with a black shawl over her face. She had deep streaks running down her face. She stood over me as I lay in bed and just looked at me.

Death is staring the dreamer in the face.

Sometimes death is thought of as taking a trip as in this dream of a sixty-six-year-old woman whose husband and son are both dead.

I am preparing to go on a trip. Although there is some reason for hurrying, I cannot force myself to move fast. I hurry from empty room to empty room looking for something.

Her days are a series of empty rooms which she is preparing to leave. She is in no hurry to make her departure for there is still a chance that she may find something to live for.

Dreams of dying turn up occasionally. Some of them are gratifying and others are horrifying. One of each type is given below, the first one that of a man in his early sixties, the second one that of a man in his middle fifties.

I dreamed that I was lying in bed feeling very tired because I had worked so hard that day. I then felt I was dying. I was happy and I was not worried about my family. I only thought that soon I would be free from worry and that I would not have to get up and go to work in the morning.

I felt that I was inside a coffin, struggling to get out. I was gasping for breath and felt I was slowly being suffocated. My efforts were extremely violent and undirected. The coffin was cold, bleak, quite ugly. It was devoid of external ornamentation and consisted only of a number of rough boards. The ground and the coffin was very cold, but I was sweating from the desperation of my efforts.

To the first dreamer, death comes as a welcome relief to the strain of worry and work. To the second dreamer, death is cold, bleak and ugly and he tries desperately to escape from its icy grip.

It is a well-known fact that as one grows older one tends to think more about the past and less about the present and future. Old people like to reminisce about "the good old days" when they were hale and hearty. By surveying dreams of successive age groups we find that this tendency to live in the past starts earlier than we ordinarily think it does. People in their thirties have very few regressive dreams while people in their forties have a considerable number, which shows that the tendency to orient toward the past begins sometime in the late thirties or early forties for the average person. We may call this point in one's life when he begins to look back the psychological midpoint of life. Before this midpoint the tension of life is dominant and accelerating. The person sees himself growing and developing, living in the midst of life, and making plans for the future. He feels that he is a vital force in an active world. After the psychological midpoint has been passed, the tension of life begins to subside while the tension of disintegration begins to accelerate. This forces him to try to recapture his old vitality by reviving the past.

This tendency to dream about the past makes another sharp spurt after the age of sixty, when the conception of growing old is verified by a number of objective signs. One really is old so that the flight into the past occurs more frequently. At the same time, an old person dreams more about death, either as something to be feared or something to be sought, because death is a reality which cannot be put off forever by living in the past.

This then is the conflict of later years—the longing for life and rejuvenation versus the desire for death and release. In dreams we see how a person tries to blend these opposing conceptions.

11   What Dreams Tell Us about Man

IN THIS final chapter let us try to weave the fabric of man's mind out of the threads which have been spun from his dreams. These dreams, bear in mind, are not the consciously contrived daydreams of waking fancy but the unconsciously fashioned night dreams of sleep. During sleep the mind expresses itself in pictures. A dream is defined, therefore, as a sequence of pictures or images which embody the ideas or conceptions of the dreamer. The goal of dream interpretation is to discover the meaning of a dream by translating images into ideas. When this task is accomplished the mind of man is exposed to public view and becomes an object of scientific study. In the last analysis dreams interest us only because they enable us to extend our knowledge of man. They tell us things about man that would be difficult to learn by any other means except by the specialized methods used in the treatment of disturbed people. Since these methods are not convenient to use in the study of a large cross-section of normal people, it devolves upon dreams to help us solve the riddle of man.

The function of dreaming as we have said many times is to reveal what is in the person's mind, not to conceal it. Dreams may appear enigmatic because they contain symbols, but these symbols are nothing more than pictorial metaphors, and like the verbal metaphors of waking life their intention is to clarify rather than to obscure thought. What is the difference between a person awake exclaiming, "He's a majestic individual," and a person asleep conjuring up the image of a king? There is no difference except in the medium of expression. The verbal metaphor expressed by the adjective "majestic" and the dream image of a king represent the same conception.

What is enigmatic about dreams is that the roots from which they grow are often buried below the surface of the conscious mind. The conscious mind is the mind which is known to us and whose contents we can talk about if we choose to. For the most part the conscious mind is filled with externals. Our awareness is an awareness of things and people and of our own bodies. We think about objective reality as it appears to us through our senses. Awake we live in a world of events and happenings so that the record of consciousness resembles nothing so much as the daily newspaper. We even persuade ourselves that if we can't talk about something it doesn't exist, or, to reverse the rule, if we can talk about it it does exist. So it comes about that the layer of the mind which represents the public world of objective reality is assumed to be the whole of the mind.

In view of this narrow conception of the mind man is bound to be puzzled by his dreams and is forced to invent fantastic explanations to account for them. If one judges the mind to encompass only the familiar thoughts of waking life, then it follows that dreams must be foreign matter which are put into the heads of sleeping persons by ancestors or gods or devils. If one prefers a less supernatural explanation he can console himself with the theory that dreams are sound and fury, signifying nothing.

There are two reasons why dreams seem to be mysterious. The first reason is that the mind of the sleeping person makes use of a relatively unfamiliar medium of expression. Most people when they are awake do not draw pictures of their ideas. They use words. Consequently they get little or no practice in expressing themselves pictorially, or in interpreting the meaning and significance of pictures. Since thinking in pictures is an unusual and unfamiliar language, it is difficult for most people to make much sense out of their dreams. If we were taught to understand the meaning of pictures as we are taught to understand the meaning of language this reason for the mystery of dreams would be abolished.

Children express themselves naturally by drawing pictures, and psychologists have found these pictures useful in exploring children's minds. It is unfortunate that this means of expression falls into disuse as we grow older if for no other reason than that we are so illiterate when it comes to understanding paintings. Even a well-educated person is ordinarily a moron in an art museum. Nor is the average person helped much by Sunday afternoon talks on art at the museum because these talks are usually about everything else save the meaning of the picture as an expression of a human mind. Line, color, design, draftsman-ship, dates, periods, incidents, gossip, schools and all the chit-chat of professional art critics and amateur art lovers are in evidence, but scarcely a word as to what the finite mind of an artist is projecting onto a canvas.

Even if by some miracle we were to become educated to the interpretation of pictures, dreams would still be unintelligible to an untrained person because they concern themselves largely with the private world of the mind, a world which lies below the surface of consciousness. Of this world the average person has very little knowledge. Hints of its existence are furnished by a consciousness of vague apprehensions and anxieties, of moods and forebodings, of restlessness and uneasiness, and of doubts and ambiguities. Like the vapors that arise from the deeper recesses of a volcanic mountain, the private regions of the mind spew forth a few visible emblems of their existence. These emblems may disturb man but he rarely of his own initiative tries to explore the regions from which these disturbances emanate. It is only within very recent times that people have made serious and systematic attempts to chart the territory of the whole mind. Chief of these explorers was Freud.

Yet how strenuously man resists acquiring this new knowl-edge of himself. Although people may appear to be fascinated by the vast wilderness within—witness the popularity of psy-chological novels, plays and books that purport to tell man about himself—few really learn anything about themselves from these sources. The vast majority of people not only reject the notion of an unconscious mind but they also feel that there is something unwholesome about probing below the surface of consciousness. "Let sleeping dogs lie." Is it not ironical that the acquiring of new knowledge should be thought to have bad consequences? Since when did knowledge become a sin and ignorance a virtue?

This resistance against knowledge has been met before in history. The astronomers met it and so have the biologists. At one time it was considered a crime to explore the inner workings of the body or to tamper with the sacred temple of the soul. Today we have pretty largely outgrown this prejudice. When we have physical symptoms we go to a doctor for amelioration of our symptoms. We think his knowledge is a wonderful thing, and we are generous in our support of medical research so that new knowledge can be acquired. We learn in school about our bodies and how to take care of them and we feel that this knowledge is a benefit and not a detriment to man's well-being.

But we learn virtually nothing about our minds in or out of school, not because the knowledge is lacking but because society has a prejudice against teaching what we know. We think it is harmful for people to learn about their minds. Even when we are mentally agitated few of us seek the help of experts, and most of us bitterly resent any suggestion that we need psychological treatment. Those of us who do consult a person who has knowledge of the mind often build up insurmountable resistances against the treatment so that no good results from it.

Civilized man might take a leaf from an isolated tribe of people living in a jungle of the Malay Peninsula. These people, the Senoi, hold the study of the mind in high esteem and their primitive psychologists are the acknowledged leaders of the tribe. They study the mind by the method of dream interpreta·tion, which is a prominent feature of a child's education and a continuing pursuit of all Senoi adults. They believe, as I do, that dreams consist of thoughts which lie below the level of consciousness during waking life and that by exploring their dreams they can learn much about themselves that they would not know otherwise.

The knowledge so acquired is acted upon in useful and constructive ways. For example, if a Senoi dreams that he is attacked by a fellow tribesman, upon awakening he will go to that person and settle his differences with him in a rational and peaceful manner. The analysis of dreams enables the Senoi to check the growth of social conflicts before they have had a chance to develop into firmly established, socially disruptive tensions. Through their understanding of all facets of the mind they are able to provide suitable outlets for the expression of personality within the framework of a democratic and responsible society. As a consequence these psychologically mature and highly selfconscious people are not plagued with war, violence or mental disease. There are no armies, jails or insane asylums in Senoi because there is no need for them.

Would it not be possible for civilized society to reach the same level of psychological maturity as the Senoi if our children were taught to assume an inquiring attitude toward the inner forces of personality and to communicate their feelings and conceptions for public discussion and guidance? By turning our eyes away from the mind do we not remain in ignorance of that which alone can give us the power to rule our destiny in creative and constructive ways? By condemning and repressing self-awareness and by encouraging and rewarding self-deception do we not build for ourselves a state of psychological illiteracy? In such a state how can man be expected to think and act rationally? The answer, of course, is that he does not. War, crime and mental disease are only part of the price he pays for his abject ignorance of the human mind.

Given this state of affairs, it is not surprising that man should consider his dreams to be quite mysterious phenomena. He has never learned about that region of the mind from which dreams come. He has never learned to look within himself as he does during sleep and to become conscious of the wilderness of conceptions which constitute the underformings of his mind.

We have described some of these underformings as they are revealed in dreams. We have seen that dreams concern themselves with material that is quite different from the contents of the daytime mind. The conceptions which appear during sleep are very personal conceptions. More than that they are ideas which for the most part do not become conscious during waking life. They are strangers to us either because we have never met them or because we have forgotten that we once knew them. Like the mechanical toys and stuffed animals of children's stories they come to life after everyone else has gone to sleep, returning to lifelessness when day returns. The analogy is not strictly accurate since the unconscious mind is hardly lifeless during the day. It is just not seen.

What are the contents of the mind as revealed in dreams? First, there is a system which contains the person's self-conceptions. These conceptions answer the question, How do I see myself? The self-conceptions of the unconscious mind often bear little resemblance to the self-deceptions of consciousness.

We may fool ourselves with trumped-up and distorted self-portraits in waking life but sleep is no friend to embellishment and illusion. Dreams are the mirror of the self.

Then there is a group of interconnected systems which embrace the person's conceptions of other people. These conceptions answer for others what the self-conceptions answer for the self. They too are often at variance with one's conscious thoughts. "You say you love your husband? Let me see your dreams."

A third system contains the conceptions of the world, what the Germans call *Weltanschauung*, a word meaning "world outlook." These conceptions attempt to personalize an impersonal world. They animate the inanimate by attributing human qualities to it. To the optimist the world is a cheerful place, while to the pessimist the same world is a cheerless place.

A fourth system consists of the conceptions of one's impulses or driving forces, the ways and means by which they are to be gratified, the obstacles which stand in the way of their fulfillment, and the penalties which are exacted when the rules governing the control of the impulses are broken.

In the fifth system of conceptions are located the conflicts. This system also has a number of intercommunicating subsystems, some of which have been described in earlier chapters. A conflict consists of opposing conceptions which war with one another for dominance. These inward struggles generate tensions and anxieties in the conscious mind. The person feels miserable without knowing why, or he attributes his worries to the wrong causes. Dreams are a faithful pictorial record of these inner conflicts and the dreamer's attempts to resolve them.

The minds of most, if not all, human beings are occupied

with five major conflicts at some time during their lives. The first of these conflicts is the conceptual struggle which a child goes through in trying to define his feelings toward his mother and father and their feelings toward him. He is pushed this way and that way by the opposing forces of love, fear and hate, and he seeks constantly to find a solution which will compose his mental turbulence. Although this conflict begins in early childhood, it maintains a stubborn hold over the mind for many years thereafter and there is even some question as to whether it ever does relax its grip completely during one's lifetime. At best this conflict probably terminates in an uneasy armistice, and may be renewed whenever the conditions are favorable. Certainly it appears to be a motivating force in the dreams of people, both young and old.

The second conflict, which is not unrelated to the first one, consists of the opposing ideas of freedom and security. This conflict also originates in childhood but reaches its climax during the late teens and early twenties. It also perseverates and may be regarded as a permanent fixture of the mind, since it is hardly likely that a person will ever obtain complete freedom or complete security, or be satisfied if he could.

These first two conflicts arise out of man's long period of immaturity during which he is a dependent member of a family group. The third conflict grows out of the androgynous nature of man as a biological entity. By nature he is both male and female, although one or the other is the dominant physical expression and is used to classify him as man or woman. The typing of individuals on the basis of distinguishing physical structures does not do away with man's inherent bisexuality. In fact the implicit denial of bisexuality which is accomplished by making a sharp division of people into two sexes aggravates the condition, because it encourages the setting up of different standards of conduct for men and women. Men are expected to act in masculine ways and women in feminine ways according to the standards of a particular society. When a man behaves like a woman or a woman like a man, he runs the risk of incurring contemptuous ridicule from his associates. Since bisexuality is the biological norm and unisexuality is the social norm, it is easily understandable why man is tormented by conflicting conceptions regarding his sex role. Both sides of his nature require satisfaction, yet society sanctions the development of only one side of his nature. Of course, many people are clever enough to find ways of outwitting the demands of society, while there are those who just ignore them, but in either case arriving at a solution involves a certain amount of stress and strain. Moreover, as dreams so clearly show, the conscious resolution of a conflict is more apparent than real since conflicts persist unconsciously even though they may have been put out of mind.

The moral conflict is essentially a conflict between biology and sociology. That is to say it is a conflict between man's animal nature and the culture's expectations regarding his conduct. As an animal, man is equipped to preserve his life by destroying his enemies and to perpetuate himself by cohabiting with a member of the opposite sex. As a socialized being, man possesses a conscience which places a stamp of approval or disapproval upon his actions. The conscience is nothing more or less than a special conceptual system which contains the person's ideas of right and wrong. These conceptions are learned through experience with the prevailing standards of the society in which the person lives.

The impulses of man come into conflict with his moral conceptions because fighting and cohabitating, except as their expression is provided for by the rules of society, are deemed to be improper modes of conduct. Morality is largely taken up with condemning sex and aggression, nor is the condemnation limited to their behavioral manifestation but also extends to their expression in thought and fancy. Since man can hardly hope to eradicate from his mind conceptions of impulses which are such an integral part of his being, and since he has a conscience imposed upon him long before he has acquired enough sagacity to integrate biological demands with sociological expectations, it follows that the moral conflict will be a constant source of trouble to him. Man may deceive himself into thinking he has fused biology with sociology when all he has really done is to repress one or the other out of immediate awareness. Dreams cut through man's conscious pretensions and show us that the moral conflict is a very provocative force in the private world of the mind.

Finally, there is that most profound of all human conflicts, the opposing vectors of life and death. In this conflict sociology plays no role. It is purely a biological drama of conflicting biological modes, the constructive, synthesizing and assimilating processes of anabolism versus the destructive, disintegrative and decomposing processes of catabolism. Anabolism or life builds to more and more complex form, catabolism or death decomposes complex forms into simpler ones. Although man is not directly aware of these biological processes unless they express themselves in easily discernible forms, as in the extremes of sickness and health, they do provide him with a constant flow of unconscious conceptions. Because of the biological tensions between anabolism and catabolism, he conceives of himself as striving to live when the anabolic vector is ascendant and as striving to die when the catabolic vector is ascendant. Our mind reflects these inner energy changes of the body as surely as they reflect the outer energy changes of the world. Indeed it is possible that the inner world always speaks with more authority than the outer world does, that sociology is ever the servant of biology. In any event the analysis of dreams gives meaning to that paradoxical assertion in the *Book of Common Prayer*, "In the midst of life we are in death."

These then are the underformings of the mind as they crop out in dreams. The foundations of the mind consist of an intricate network of conceptual systems which develop out of man's nature as a biological energy system and his status as a receptacle of culture.

Now let us address ourselves to a question that must be in the mind of every reader. What bearing do these conceptual underformings have upon the actions of a person? Do the innermost thoughts in the labyrinth of the mind make their effects known in behavior? What is the connection, if any, between the unconscious and man's conduct?

The answer which is favored by observation and experiment is that the unconscious exercises a considerable selective influence on one's behavior. Given a wide range of behavior possibilities, the particular mode of action which is adopted is dictated by the conceptual systems of the person. His conduct like his dreams is a manifestation of inner mental states, or as Emerson said, "The event is the actualizing of thought." Deeds and dreams are both in a sense metaphors or symbols of the mind. For example, if a young man conceives of older men as enemies and if he thinks that the way to cope with them is to be submissive, these ideas will be embodied in his behavior. He will be deferential to his father, to male teachers, to bosses and to other older men who enter his life. What appears to be a habitual mode of conduct is, in this case, merely the expression of a persistent set of conceptions which direct his behavior in a consistent way. His deference symbolizes an idea of which he may be totally unaware.

Another young man may harbor the idea of rebellion against older men, in which case his behavior will be characterized by rebelliousness. This conception may be acted out in a variety of ways. A boy wrecks his father's car and it is found that this is an unconscious act of aggression against the father. A student refuses to learn because he hates the teacher. Workers rebel against the boss by going out on strike. Criminals and other anti-social persons may regulate their whole lives in accordance with the idea of rebellion.

Or consider the contrasting world views of two people who supposedly live in the same world. One of them conceives of the world as a friendly place. In his relations with people, he is friendly, co-operative, helpful and courteous. The other conceives of the world as a hostile place. In his interpersonal conduct he is unfriendly, competitive, selfish and unmannerly. Let these two people meet and they understand one another as little as though they came from different planets. They cannot communicate with one another because their conceptual systems are so different.

Remember the young man whose dreams revealed that he had contrasting conceptions of women. Guided by the conception that women are pure, sublimated beings, his conduct, we would predict, would be characterized by tenderness and thoughtfulness. Guided by the other conception that women are aggressively sexual, his behavior would be crude and thoughtless. Now suppose that this lad was observed by one person when the first conception was directing his behavior and by another person when the second conception was in control. Do you suppose that the descriptions given by these two observers would coincide? Not at all. To all intents and purposes, the two observers might as well have been describing two different people.

Recall also the young man whose dreams presented a picture of desertion and loneliness. Under what conditions did these conceptions appear? They appeared in his dreams whenever he gave in to his impulses or rebelled against authority. His feeling of utter despair resulted from the severity of his conscience whenever he attempted to have a good time or be independent. What kind of behavior would we expect him to display in waking life? We would expect him to be a model person, one who avoids temptation and seeks the wisdom of other people's advice. This is the kind of behavior he actually manifests. Neither he nor his associates know that his exemplary deportment is controlled by an immense fear of being ostracized by society if he should stray from the path of righteousness. We know it because we have read his dreams.

If one adopts the view that man's behavior is determined to a

great extent by ideas which reside in the basements and attics
of the mind, a good deal of behavior which we find puzzling
makes sense. Why, for example, do we instinctively dislike some
people when we first meet them? May it not be because the
person we meet reminds us unwittingly of another person? The
resemblance may be nothing more than a wrinkle under the
eyes, a slight distention of the nostrils, an almost invisible curl
of the lips, or an inclination of the head, but it is enough to
reinstate the same feeling of antagonism toward the new person
that we feel toward the other individual.

Falling in love is another strange phenomenon. Why does it
occur so suddenly and so unexpectedly? It can even happen while
we are walking along the street and see in the crowd a person
who fills our heart with love, even though we may never see the
person again. Why did we pick out just that person from among
so many to fall in love with? May it not be a shock of unconscious recognition of someone we used to love, a reincarnated
conception which has been buried for years in a forgotten cup-
board of the mind? Perhaps the person we love so suddenly is a
reincarnation of our father or mother, or possibly a brother or
sister. Or perhaps Narcissuslike we fall in love with one whose
image is a reflection of our own self-image. Has it not often
been remarked that some husbands and wives resemble one
another so closely that they are taken for brother and sister, or
that a man marries a woman who is like his mother and a woman
marries a man who is like her father? These things do not
happen by chance.

Nothing happens by chance. A person dreams that he is hurt
in an accident and we discover by analyzing the dream that he is

punishing himself for a misdeed. Why then should we be surprised to find that a person who hurts himself in waking life is
acting out an idea of atonement? Is not an event always an
actualizing of an unconscious thought?

We all know why an old maid looks under the bed at night.
Are not many of our fears based upon the same principle, that
what is on our mind might come true? We warn a person who
is handling a sharp knife to be careful. Before warning him
have we not had an image of his being cut, so that the warning
serves to prevent *our* idea from being actualized in *his* behavior?

Unconscious guiding principles influence our choice of a
vocation. A person who has learned to conceive of the world in
terms of order, number, measure, balance and precision will find
the engineering profession attractive because engineering conceives of the world in the same manner. Another person will
prefer the legal profession because his ideas run along the lines
of verbal combat, oral inquisitions and dramatic exhibitionism.
The dominant conceptions of truck drivers are power, speed,
energy and physical aggression. Among the tens of thousands of
occupations available to people, each person chooses the one
which he thinks best fits his particular conceptual framework.

A person cannot do anything without expressing some aspect
of his personal ideology. The clothes he selects, the books he
reads, the hobbies he cultivates, the entertainment he seeks, the
candidates he votes for—in every department of life man reacts
selectively to his world in terms of his conceptual systems. Even
such a simple task as estimating the size of coins bears the im-
print of one's personal convictions. Poor children, who value
money more highly than rich children do, actually think coins

are larger than they really are. In a similar vein, people who are hungry have more thoughts of food, talk about food and see more food objects in their environment than do people who are not hungry. The extreme case is that of hallucinations, in which a person is under the influence of such a strong idea that he builds the world in the image of that idea.

It is clear from these many examples that man's conduct is the visible embodiment of his conceptions, that behavior is the shadowing forth of deeply recessed mental states. During sleep, when the mind turns in upon itself, these recesses are explored and charted in the shape of dreams. Dreams, in effect, provide us with maps of regions which are inaccessible in waking consciousness. With these maps we are better able to follow the course of man's behavior, to understand why he selects one road rather than another, to anticipate the difficulties and obstacles he will encounter, and to predict his destinations.

One final question and then we are through. Where do the underformings of the mind come from? This is a large question the full answer to which still lies beyond the frontiers of man's knowledge. There are those who believe that the basic furnishings of the mind are a legacy of man's ancestral history. According to this view the foundations of mind are present at birth and from the very beginning of life exercise a selective influence upon man's experiences. For example, man's fear of the dark is inherited from ancestors who were exposed to the dangers of the night because they did not know how to make light. This theory is difficult to prove or disprove by the methods of science.

Then there are those, including this writer, who believe that the groundwork of mind is laid down during the early years of life, probably during the first two years. In this period of time, the baby has experiences which supply him with prototypic conceptions. A prototypic conception is one which serves as a model or pattern for building other conceptions. It steers the mind along a definite developmental course, selecting ideas that are consistent with the prototype and rejecting or ignoring ideas that are at odds with the prototype. For example, a baby learns by eating to expect pleasure from stimulation of the mouth and lips. Thereafter when he is disturbed or tense he seeks relief by bringing things to the mouth or by using the mouth. This is the prototypic conception upon which a great deal of later behavior is based—thumb-sucking, smoking, kissing, drinking and talking to name only a few. Cases of obesity due to over-eating have been traced to the dominance of this conception. Fat people find relief in eating when they are emotionally upset. It is interesting that people who leave off smoking or drinking often put on weight because eating is a substitute for the abandoned habit. The primary cause of alcoholism is the prototypic conception that one can avoid pain and find pleasure by taking in something through the mouth. There is a close resemblance between the baby with a bottle and the drunkard with a bottle, inasmuch as both are finding pleasure through oral stimulation.

A multitude of other prototypic conceptions get built into the mind during these early years. What is done to the baby overshadows in importance anything that is done to the person in later life. We sometimes imagine that because the baby is immature and does not appear to notice what is going on in the world that these early experiences are not very permanent. Yet just because the baby cannot react to his experiences by talking about them or showing others what they mean to him should not blind us to the fact that they often make indelible impressions upon his mind. After all, the infant, since he is a plastic and malleable energy system, is very easily marked, and markings once made are hard to erase. First experiences are significant because they have priority over later ones.

These prototypic conceptions become overlaid by the ideas acquired in later life so that often it is difficult to trace adult conceptions back to their original source. The contribution which dreams make to the understanding of man is that they reveal the substratum of his mind, the original prototypes of which his later ideas are derivatives.

In looking back over what we have written in this book it strikes us that we have presented a rather gloomy picture of man. We have talked a great deal about his conflicts and anxieties, his perplexities and predicaments, and scarcely at all about man's joys and accomplishments. In a sense this is not our fault since we have let the dreams of man fashion their own picture of him. Our role has been that of interpreter, not creator. We have tried to put in everything about man that we have found in his dreams, without distorting, exaggerating or concealing the actual picture.

The fact of the matter is that dreams do not have much to say about the joys and accomplishments of man. Nor is this to be accounted for by the kind of people whose dreams have been studied. Our informants are not neurotic individuals. They are not social misfits or psychiatric patients. They are, on the whole, an accomplished, capable group of people who have had more than their share of successes and gratifications in life. As a group they are probably pretty much like the readers of this book.

Dreams of successful achievement are rare because our accomplishments do not provide the mind with energy and tension. An accomplishment represents a reduction of tension, and without tension there is no thinking and no dreaming. Since we only dream when there is a problem to dream about it follows that our dreams are more concerned with the complexities of life than with its simplicities. In fact when we run across a dream series which is replete with simple wish fulfillment we suspect that the dreamer is indulging in magical thinking. He is evading his problems instead of facing them.

There is a positive side to this depressing dream picture of man. After all, man cannot solve his problems unless he recognizes them for what they are and then tries to think his way through to rational solutions. Nothing is to be gained and a lot may be lost by glossing over the very real contradictions which exist in man. We certainly cannot cause these contradictions to disappear by drugging our minds with sentimental moonshine and happy endings.

Throughout history man has displayed considerable creativity in mastering problems of existence and in discovering the secrets of the physical world. By using his intelligence he has made the world a more comfortable place in which to live. The accomplishments of science and technology are among the most notable achievements of the human mind. Nor has man ever quailed for long before the immensity of the problems facing him. Goaded on by insatiable curiosity, man has penetrated deeper and deeper into the nature of the material environment.

When he is asleep and dreaming his mind is occupied with other kinds of problems than those of the external world. Dreams attempt to solve the inner problems of the person himself. Dreaming like all thinking is essentially a creative process, and not a soporific one as daydreaming is. Dreams are the products of good hard thought and it is too bad that man ignores them as he does.

We suggest that man begin to pay attention to his dreams and that he learn to use them as the starting point for additional creative thinking about his personal problems. If he would give as much thought to himself during the day as he does during the night, man might deepen his self-knowledge to the point where he could master his conflicts instead of being mastered by them. For it is only by being completely self-conscious that man can be rational and wise in all of his undertakings.

APPENDIX. Notes and Comments

The following notes are provided for the reader who may wish to do further reading on the psychology of dreams or who may want to check original sources from which I have drawn material. I have also interspersed comments and evaluations which represent my thoughts on a number of matters relating to dreams and people who write about dreams. The page and line numbers preceding each note refer to the page and line in the text which is being annotated.

CHAPTER I.

Page 1, Line 2. For an anthology of what people throughout the ages have written about dreams we are indebted to the careful scholarship of Ralph L. Woods. His anthology, *The World of Dreams* (Random House, 1947), contains two hundred excerpts from the writings of savants, scientists, anthropologists, literary figures, and psychologists who have had something to say about dreams. We can read Coleridge's account of the dream that inspired the writing of the poem "Kubla Khan" and Robert Louis Stevenson's testimony regarding the dreams which inspired some of his writings. Abraham Lincoln's prophetic dream of his own death several days before he was assassinated is recounted by his good friend Ward Lamon. *The World of Dreams* makes fascinating reading, and its usefulness to the writer on dreams cannot be overestimated. Indeed, one recent writer of a book on dreams seems to have taken his long chapter on the history of dream interpretation almost entirely from Woods' anthology without giving Woods appropriate credit. He even misspells Woods' name!

A recent book which contains a very stimulating and scholarly chapter on the attitudes of the ancient Greeks toward their dream experiences is *The Greeks and the Irrational* by E. R. Dodds (University of California Press, 1951).

Page 1, Line 4. The first edition of Freud's *Interpretation of Dreams* appeared in 1900. Not only did it prove to be the greatest book on dreams ever to be written, but it has also become recognized as an intellectual landmark of modern thought. It ushered in the century of psychological man, a century in which man began to pay closer attention to his own nature and to seek to know himself. Freud himself accurately assessed the importance of *The Interpretation of Dreams* when in the foreword to the third English edition (1931) he wrote, "It contains, even according to my present-day judgment, the most valuable of all the discoveries it has been my good fortune to make. Insight such as this falls to one's lot but once in a lifetime." *The Interpretation of Dreams* is included in *The Basic Writings of Sigmund Freud* (Random House, 1938). Unfortunately Brill, the editor of this volume, decided to omit most of the first chapter in which Freud reviews the history of dream theory.

It is well known that Jung, an early disciple of Freud's, broke with him over theoretical issues, notably Freud's pansexualism. Jung is the great exponent of symbolism, and he believes that symbols are the key to an understanding of man's mental development. The bedrock upon which a person's mind is formed consists of the accumulated experiences of the past. In other words Jung believes in inherited ideas which are the common property of all men. These inherited ideas constitute the collective unconscious from which so many of our dreams come. But dreams look forward as well as backward, Jung believes. They contain glimpses of the future psychological development of the individual, and so by heeding their messages one can plan an appropriate course of action. Jung's ideas regarding dreams are presented in his *Analytical Psychology* (1916) and his *Psychology of the Unconscious* (1916).

Among psychoanalytic writers, it is Wilhelm Stekel who most assiduously elaborated Freud's dream theory. Although his two-volume work, *The Interpretation of Dreams* (Liveright, 1943), does not approach Freud's book for profundity, close and orderly reasoning, or scientific cautiousness, it makes interesting reading. Stekel had a pyrotechnical mind. His ideas burst forth like Roman candles and skyrockets, and often as not they burn out as quickly as fireworks on a July evening. Freud said of Stekel that he "injured psychoanalysis as much as he has benefited it."

Page 1, Line 13. I would like to acknowledge my debt to the many hundreds of students in my classes who helped me collect dreams. In performing this great service they were both serious and punctilious. Thanks to them I believe that I now possess the largest collection of dreams of normal people in existence. Although I do not have an exact count, my files contain more than ten thousand individual dreams. In collecting dreams I use a printed form, copies of which are available on request.

Page 2, Line 3. Emerson's views on dreams are found in his essay, "Demonology," part of which is reprinted in Woods, *The World of Dreams.*

Page 2, Line 7. Although Stekel used the dream series method, I was not aware of this fact until after I had hit upon it myself. My first published account of the dream series method appeared in the *Journal of Social and Abnormal Psychology*, January, 1947, under the title "Diagnosing Personality by the Analysis of Dreams."

Boss, a Swiss psychiatrist, has used the dream series method to trace the course of deterioration and improvement in mental patients. He finds that during mental deterioration dreams become more coarsely sexual and less symbolized and that during remission of the psychosis dreams become more highly symbolized.

Page 4, Line 5. This story and many similar ones are recounted in Woods, *The World of Dreams.*

Page 4, Line 24. The notion that dreams are caused by retinal processes independent of external stimulation was put forth by the physiological psychologist, George Trumbull Ladd, in 1892. His theory will be found in Woods, *The World of Dreams,* Page 511.

Page 4, Line 27. This account of Hobbes' theory of dreams is based upon an excerpt from *Leviathan* which appears in Woods' anthology.

Page 5, Line 9. The reference is, of course, to a best-seller of 1948, *Sexual Behavior in the Human Male* by A. C. Kinsey, W. B. Pomeroy, and C. E. Martin (W. B. Saunders, 1948).

Page 6, Line 9. This study was reported by M. W. Calkins in the *Journal of American Psychology,* April, 1893.

Page 6, Line 25. This example is taken from the work of Dr. D. B. Klein which is reported in the University of Texas Bulletin, No. 3009, March, 1930, under the title *Experimental Production of Dreams During Hypnosis.* Many similar experiments have been made. These are reviewed and evaluated by Freud in his *Interpretation of Dreams.*

Page 7, Line 24. My theory of dreams is presented in detail in an article to appear in the *Journal of General Psychology,* entitled "A Cognitive Theory of Dreams."

Page 15, Line 10. The dream narratives which appear in this book are printed just as they were written down by the dreamer. They have not been changed in any way. Consequently, the grammar is not always perfect.

CHAPTER 2.

Page 21, Line 11. I have reported these findings in greater detail in an article, "What People Dream About," in the *Scientific American,* May, 1951.

Page 21, Line 12. Actually we use a fifth category, plot. Dream plots are discussed in later chapters under the heading of inner conflicts, since the plot of a dream is motivated by a conflict.

Page 45, Line 27. One of my students, Dr. Robert Fortier, wrote a doctoral dissertation on the topic of color in dreams, *A Study of the*

Relation of the Response to Color and Some Personality Functions (Western Reserve University Library, 1952).

CHAPTER 3.

Page 48, Line 20. Quoted from *Sexual Behavior in the Human Male* by A. C. Kinsey, W. B. Pomeroy, and C. E. Martin.

Page 54, Line 1. It is interesting and perhaps significant that the Greek word for ladder or staircase is *klimax* which is the source for the English word *climax*, a term that is used to denote the sexual orgasm.

Julian Green, the distinguished novelist, has commented upon the significance of staircases in his novels.

In all my books, the conception of fear or of any other of the stronger forms of emotion seems in some unaccountable way to be connected with a staircase. I noticed this yesterday, when I was thinking over the novels I have written. For example, in *le Voyageur*, the old Colonel's going upstairs is connected in the hero's mind with a sort of rising of fear. In *Mont-Cinère*, Emily meets her father's ghost on the stairs. In Adrienne Mesurat, the heroine causes her father to have a fall on the staircase, where she then spends part of the night. In *Léviathan*, Mme. Grosgeorge, in an agony of mind, goes up and down the stairs. In *les Clefs de la mort*, it is on the stairs that the hero thinks out the murder he is to commit. In *l'Autre Sommeil*, the hero faints on a staircase. In Epaves, there is the staircase on which Philip remains while in a state of indecision, and watches for his wife. And lastly, in the story which I am finishing, a staircase is the scene of a sinister outburst of wild laughter. I wonder how I have been able to repeat this effect so often without noticing that I have done so. When I was a child I used to dream that I was being pursued on a staircase. My mother had the same fears in the days of her youth, and I may to some extent have inherited them.

Personal Record (Harpers, 1939)

It is of interest to observe that a father figure appears as the central character in several of these incidents, and suggests that Green's fear of staircases is based upon some forgotten or repressed experience connected with his father. His memoirs reveal that he felt strongly attached to his mother, who died when he was fourteen, and hostile toward his father, a feeling which he seems to have repressed successfully. As a child he did not like to go upstairs to bed because it meant separation from his beloved mother, and so he devised various schemes to get his mother to come up to his room and stay with him. Often she would give in and then Julian's father would remonstrate with her for babying the boy. Thus, a deep feeling for his mother, fear of losing her, and hostility toward the father, became associated in Julian's mind with "going upstairs to bed."

Page 70, Line 25. Many readers will take issue with the statement that "sex and aggression are the two basic motivating forces of thought and behavior." For my part I cannot understand man's conduct unless I start with this as *the* fundamental fact of human nature. Everything else is derivative. Sex and aggression are responsible not only for the worst in man but also for the best. When we learn how to channel man's sexual and aggressive drives into individually and socially constructive outlets, we will have achieved utopia.

CHAPTER 4.

Page 85, Line 15. Numerous readers will disagree with my statement that dreams do not foretell the future, yet I must in fairness to the evidence and to logic contradict the popular belief that dreams are omens. Of course some things we dream do come true, but many more do not. Those that come true stick in our mind while those that do not are quickly forgotten.

At the time of the kidnapping of the Lindbergh child, two Harvard psychologists, Henry Murray and D. R. Wheeler, conducted the following investigation. In March, 1932, a few days after the kidnapping but before the baby's body had been found, a request for dreams relative to the kidnapping appeared in papers throughout the country and brought in over 1,300 dream. The dreams were compared with the facts as they were later established, namely that the baby's *mutilated* and *naked* body was discovered in a *shallow grave*, in some *woods*, near a *road* several miles away from the Lindbergh home, and that *death* had been instantaneous. In approximately five per cent of the dreams sent in before the fact of the baby's death had been established, the baby appeared to be dead, and in *seven* dreams, the actual location of the body, its nakedness and the manner of its burial were more or less accurately portrayed. The following dream is the most faithful of the seven:

I thought I was standing or walking in a very muddy place among many trees. One spot looked as though it might be a round, shallow grave. Just then I heard a voice saying, "The baby has been murdered and buried there." I was so frightened that I immediately awoke.

Only four of the seven dreams included the three items: death, burial in a grave, and location among trees.

Are these seven dreams prophetic and clairvoyant? Or is it just coincidence that these seven dreams out of thirteen hundred should have got some of the details correct? We would need to know the probabilities, as the authors state, of the child being either dead or alive; and if dead, whether in water, above ground or below ground and whether inside a house, out in an open field or in the woods. Although the authors acknowledge that they do not have the data for estimating these probabilities, they feel that *more than seven* out of thirteen hundred dreams should have made reference to these critical features on the basis of chance alone.

The fact that only five per cent of the dreams pictured the baby as being dead is itself a strong argument against the validity of prophetic dreams. It suggests rather that the desire to have the baby alive (wish fulfillment) is the determining factor for the 1,300 dreamers. In any event, there is little evidence in this study to support the notion that dreams are prophetic.

A report of the Murray-Wheeler investigation will be found in the *Journal of Psychology*, 1937.

Page 87, Line 12. After the manuscript of this book was completed, I received a letter from Iceland which contained a novel explanation of dreams. According to the writer dreams are put into our minds by beings living on other planets. Interplanetary communication by this view is already an established fact rather than a mere dream of scientists!

CHAPTER 5.

Page 90, Line 14. For a stimulating and scholarly account of dream books of the past and present the reader is referred to an article entitled "Oneirocritica Americana" by H. B. Weiss in the *Bulletin of the New York Public Library*, 1944. Mr. Weiss was able to purchase fifty-seven dream books which are currently sold in New York City.

Page 93, Line 9. Perhaps the best example of a psychoanalytic dream book is E. A. Gutheil's *The Language of the Dream* (Macmillan, 1939).

Page 95, Line 11. A more detailed presentation of my theory of dream symbols is to appear in the *Journal of General Psychology* under the title "A Cognitive Theory of Dream Symbolism."

Page 97, Line 15. I have borrowed this example, as well as many of the ideas expressed in this chapter, from Susanne Langer's *Philosophy in a New Key* (Penguin Books, 1948). I consider Mrs. Langer's book to be the best study of symbolism which has been made.

Page 105, Line 7. A comparison of the interpretation of dream series with and without free associations was made by one of my students, Dr. Walter Reis, for a doctoral dissertation. He found that dream series without free association yielded just about as much information concerning the personality of the dreamer as dream series with free associations. His thesis, *Comparison of Personality Variables Derived from Dream Series with and without Free Associations*, is on file in the Western Reserve University Library.

CHAPTER 6.

Page 126, Line 17. For a comprehensive treatment of the Oedipus complex see P. Mullahy's *Oedipus: Myth and Complex* (Hermitage, 1948).

CHAPTER 7.

Page 128, Line 1. There is a third way of life according to Saul Rosenzweig. It is the way of interdependence. This is the ideal way in a truly democratic society.

CHAPTER 8.

Page 152, Line 1. That the good person who is tempted but does not yield feels guiltier than the transgressor is borne out by a study made by Donald MacKinnon. He found that students who did not cheat on a test felt more remorse than those who did. Their remorse was due to a consciously felt temptation to cheat. See D. W. MacKinnon, "Violation of Prohibitions" in H. A. Murray's *Explorations in Personality* (Oxford University Press, 1938).

CHAPTER 9.

Page 169, Line 12. The dreams of women are influenced by the menstrual cycle. During the first half of the menstrual cycle when the sex hormone is most active, women tend to have erotic dreams. During the second half of the menstrual cycle when the maternal hormone comes to the fore, their dreams become maternal in character. These are the findings of T. Benedek and B. B. Rubenstein which are reported in the Psychosomatic Medicine Monographs, Numbers 1 and 2 for 1942.

Page 169, Line 29. For a comprehensive discussion of sex differences see A. Scheinfeld's *Women and Men* (Harcourt, Brace, 1944).

Page 193, Line 7. For a sympathetic and valid portrayal of homosexuality as it appears in an adolescent I recommend Fritz Peters' novel *Finistère* (Farrar, Straus, 1951).

CHAPTER 10.

Page 195, Line 3. Freud postulated that man has a death wish as well as a life wish in an essay entitled *Beyond the Pleasure Principle* (1920). Even among Freud's most loyal followers the notion of a death wish is not widely accepted. Yet, to me, it represents the zenith of Freud's thinking.

Page 207, Line 14. Whitman is not the only poet who has written of death. In fact, the two major themes of great literature are love and death. Romeo and Juliet is the prototype par excellence.

Page 209, Line 27. The fact that we often dream of people who are dead is probably responsible in part for the belief that dreams are messages from one's ancestors.

CHAPTER 11.

Page 218, Line 28. This account of the Senoi is taken from an article by Kilton Steward entitled "Dream Theory in Malaya" which appeared in the fall, 1951, issue of *Complex*.

Page 220, Line 6. "That since wars begin in the minds of men, it is in the minds of men that the defences of peace must be constructed." This is the first sentence of the preamble of the UNESCO charter.

Page 229, Line 24. I was told recently by a psychologist doing research for an advertising firm that one can tell a lot about a person knowing the brand of cigarette he smokes.

Page 229, Line 27. The reference for this study is J. S. Bruner and C. C. Goodman, "Value and Need as Organizing Factors in Perception," *Journal of Abnormal and Social Psychology,* 1947.

Index

Catalog

If you are interested in a list of fine Paperback
books, covering a wide range of subjects
and interests, send your name and address,
requesting your free catalog, to:

McGraw-Hill Paperbacks
1221 Avenue of Americas
New York, N. Y. 10020